SAM CHAND

YOUR NEXT BOLD MOVE

MAKING DECISIONS
IN TIMES OF TRANSITION

Your Next Bold Move:
Making Decisions in Times of Transition

by Sam Chand
copyright ©2017

originally published as *Who Moved Your Ladder,* by Sam
Chand with Cecil Murphey

trade paperback ISBN: 978-1-943294-66-4
cover design by Vanessa Mendozzi

CONTENTS

CHAPTER ONE
WHO MOVED MY LADDER?

I'M A VISIONARY; you probably are too. That's why you're reading this book. We are visionaries because we have a dream. We're willing to throw everything into fulfilling that desire. It's our driving force. We pray fervently, think constantly, daydream frequently, and regularly envision what life will be like up ahead. We may not know where we'll end up, but we know the direction we're headed.

In my previous book, *Who's Holding Your Ladder*, I used the symbol of a ladder to explain the vision. If the ladder is the vision, we are the climbers; we are the ones with a burning zeal. Ladder holders are those who support and help to implement our vision. We never want to forget that our success as a visionary greatly depends on the quality of our ladder holders. We also need different holders as our ladder (vision) extends higher.

When I used that symbol, I referred to what we believe we're called to do and a way to look ahead and see where we're going. Climbing the ladder is our onward pursuit of that as-yet-unfulfilled dream.

In this book, I want to use the same symbols, but now we'll look at the ladder differently. We had the vision—we knew where we wanted to go and we climbed faithfully and finally reached most or all of our goals.

After we've reached the top of the ladder, we reach the time of transition. After all, in life nothing is permanent. For example, one day I realized I had climbed the ladder of success as the president of a growing Bible College. For fourteen years, I had dreamed and worked hard as I ascended that golden ladder. I loved the people, the work, the challenges, and the excitement of going up each rung. One day, however, something changed. (I write "one day" but something had been going on for months until the day I became aware.)

"Who moved my ladder? This isn't where I want to stay," I said. As I was to learn, many leaders are or have been exactly where I stood that day. Who moved our ladders? Who changed things? Who took away the excitement? The joy? The challenge?

The truth is, where I stood on my ladder was exactly where I had wanted to go—at least it was when I started up that particular ladder. What I had to face—and so do many of us—is that it may appear as if someone has moved our ladder. The excitement, joy, and challenge dissipate. We look over our shoulder and realize where we were when we first felt those giddy emotions and rushed up those rungs. Those were the days when we jumped out of bed every morning. Even at night when we put our weary bodies to bed, we felt as if we had accomplished something. We knew we were moving in the right direction; we had climbed a little higher on the ladder.

When that level of enthusiasm begins to drain, here's the reality we have to face: No one has moved our ladder. It's in exactly the same place where it has always been. We have changed. We climbed the ladder—and it may have been the right one—but it's no longer the preferred or fulfilling one. At least, that was my experience.

Some may have climbed high on ladders, and as they neared the top they said, "Oh, this isn't really where I wanted to go." It makes me think of something the late Joseph Campbell said when he spoke of following our bliss—our passion. He said that most of us follow the expedient way, what he calls the right-hand path and we climb the ladder in front of us. When we get to the top, we realize that we've had our ladder resting against the wrong wall. The left-handed path is riskier, but that's the path of bliss.

In my case, it hadn't been the wrong wall; however, it would have been the wrong wall had I continued to stay. My ladder had moved. That is, my vision had changed.

Before I go any further, I want to tell you a little about climbing my ladder.

●●●

The year 1989 changed everything for me; that year I became president of Beulah Heights Bible College in Atlanta, Georgia. That position was the most exciting one I'd ever had. It was like climbing a dream ladder. It wasn't quite like walking on streets of gold in the New Jerusalem—but it felt close.

As I started up the first rungs, I often paused to thank God for putting me in that situation, for giving me the opportunity to dream big, and to have the backing to put those dreams into effect. The school began to grow, and I saw even greater potential for us. I frequently discovered new opportunities and began doing things that other schools hadn't even thought of. We not only trained Christian leaders, but we found ways to affect our community as well.

I went up one rung at a time and loved every step. The higher I ascended the more wonderful my life seemed. "I could

7

keep this the rest of my life," I said with a smile. Every morning I awakened, eager to tackle the challenges. Everywhere I looked, I saw progress.

One day, however, I surveyed the world from my ladder. The passion had diminished. I didn't hate my ladder or what I was doing. It felt, well, a bit predictable, even a little boring. "I've done this before," I said.

"What's wrong with me?" That's the question most of us ask ourselves when the thrill of our jobs subsides. Surely, there was something wrong with me. If something had become defective, I had to figure out what part malfunctioned, fix it, and move on. As I pondered that question, I realized that I had been standing in about the same place for several months. Activities had not stopped—I had set things up so that no one noticed my standing still. But I noticed.

More important, off and on for months I searched and beat up on myself for having lost my cutting-edge enthusiasm. Somewhere in the process, however, I slowly admitted that I wasn't the problem: The problem was the ladder.

What had happened to the beautiful, wonderful ladder I had been climbing? Where was the excitement I had felt as I slowly ascended? Where was the inner contentment and joy? Why was there no constant excitement as I stared at the next rung?

What's happened? Who had moved my golden ladder? Was it time to find a new ladder? Was it time to hang on, grit my teeth, and just keep doing what I'd been doing for more than a decade? Or was it time to climb off my ladder and find a new one?

It was a time of transition—but it took me weeks to accept that fact.

That's the context in which I write.

This is a book about transitions—about moving from one position to another. Some people have to move. They're laid off, fired, or told, "Find a different job." They're forced to make changes. But how do we go about making transitions when...

- all is going well?
- when we're successful?
- we've achieved more than we ever dreamed?
- our friends and critics still applaud our achievements?

I had climbed higher on the ladder than anyone had expected. After I reached the top rung, I realized something: I had gone as far as I could on this ladder. I had to think about where I was and where I wanted to go next. If it was time to switch ladders, which one do I climb? Was it time to relax, rest, stand and survey what I had done and enjoy it?

Most leaders face that situation sometime in their careers-and some more than once. It's not a comfortable place in which to stand.

• • •

I began my search for resources to assist me in my transitional decision making. Here are some of the issues I struggled with:

- What is going on?
- Why was I excited and scared at the same time?
- What are the critical questions I need to ask?
- What are the essential ingredients?
- What about a successor?

To my amazement and dismay, I found little information available. That's the major reason I've written this book. I want to help others as they make their next bold move.

CHAPTER TWO

GODLY DISCONTENT: GETTING COUNSEL

D
ON'T EVER MAKE HIGH-LEVEL TRANSITIONS," I urge leaders, "until you have come face to face with yourself." Another way to say it is that before leaders leave a position, they need to ask—and honestly answer—this question: What is the internal health of my organization or church?

By that, I refer to the present location, present size, relational levels, and professional competence of our organization. Are we healthy on the inside? Years ago, someone told me, "Always leave on a high note." That was excellent advice. Whether it's the role of the pastor or the CEO of an organization, if there is a choice, don't leave when things are down. Too often leaders vacate for the wrong reasons. Too often, they're running from problems. Rather than staying and working through them and bringing the organization to a winning situation again, they switch ladders.

"If they run once," I've heard it said, "they'll run every time difficulties strike." Of course, there are situations where leaders feel they must leave, such as the pressure of the board to resign. Sometimes it's the Peter Principle in action: I have risen to the highest level of my incompetence. When I know I can't do an adequate job in my present position, leaving may be one of the wisest things I can do for the organization.

In my own case, I was the president of Beulah Heights Bible College and had been there fourteen years. Although I chose to leave, it wasn't an easy decision for me. In this book, I want to take readers through the various steps I followed. Although my situation is unique, I believe the principles and experiences apply to any of us who choose to leave a successful position, whether CEO, pastor, manager, or a church elder.

In my case, it began with what I call godly discontent. I had worked hard to help the college move forward—and it had happened. I had met each goal and every challenge that confronted me. Instead of feeling joyful and excited, boredom set in. Most leaders go after challenges—whether growing a church or developing an organization, adding staff, boosting productivity, or increasing finances. When we've done that, we begin to feel like Alexander the Great. One legend says that once he had conquered the then-known world, he sat down and cried. He had no more worlds to conquer.

My world wasn't that vast or my accomplishments that great, but I had done more than I had set out to do. Boredom had begun to creep into my life. I'd stare at my desk calendar and sigh. "I've done all this before." As one of my friends said of himself in a similar situation, "I had no more mountains to climb." The thrill of adventure had gone. I kept doing more of what I had done before.

One morning I awoke, and I thought about my already scheduled activities for that day: a breakfast meeting at 7:30; three morning appointments; lunch with a potential donor for the school; a report to write for the board meeting the following week; and that night I would speak at a large church that had decided to hold extension classes. I sat down on my bed and wished I could call in sick. I had worked hard to make such events happen and now that they were realities, I had to fight boredom. Not everyone listens to that internal boredom.

For some, the discontent forces them to increase their activity and struggle to recapture the thrill of success. For a short time, I tried to do just that. I thought the answer was doing more. After a few weeks, I realized that "more" didn't mean greater enjoyment or excitement. "More" simply meant I was busier. How did I regain that enthusiasm? For weeks, I pondered my dilemma. I didn't talk about it, because I didn't know how to talk about it.

That was the beginning of a godly dissatisfaction—even though I didn't know to label it that way.

There were things I did—and did well—but something within me whispered, "I don't want to continue doing the same things again and again." As I listened to my inner groanings, I admitted that I didn't want to do more administration. I was tired of fundraising. Dealing with staff issues began to tire me. I didn't want to do conflict management any more. I didn't want to schedule more meetings, breakfasts, or accept more preaching opportunities. I cringed at the thought of having to conduct one more job interview. I didn't want to deal with the financial aspects of our school—even though we were in a healthy situation. Those were typical of the things I had to face that I didn't want to do any more.

Inner boredom. That's what afflicted me and even once I admitted it to myself, I kept it hidden from others. "I can handle all the job demands in my sleep," I said aloud. I could do those things—and I had been doing them for fourteen years—but I just didn't want to do them any longer. As long as I focused on what was wrong with me, I got nowhere. Once I opened myself to the possibility of God, I knew I was moving in the right direction.

What if my dissatisfaction is from God? What if this is the first step toward disengaging myself from the old to prepare me for the new? That's when I understood the concept of godly dissatisfaction. It meant I was all right and no matter how much effort I forced, I would grow even more disenchanted.

I had to switch ladders, but I didn't know which ladder to grab. There were many of them out there, and I could have started climbing any of them.

Before I could move to a new ladder, I had to be certain I didn't want to stay in my present position. Almost every day I argued with myself. At first, I was too scared to seriously contemplate leaving. I had worked hard, earned the respect of my peers, and—for the first time in my life—had brought financial stability into my life. I could stay in my present position until my retirement.

Or could I?

One day I came face to face with my need to change. It may not sound like much, but I had a couple of hours between meetings in Omaha, Nebraska. My assistant Erick Moon and I walked through the Old Market while I casually moved from stall to stall, fascinated with the place, but not wanting to buy anything. Then I spotted an original greeting card. I stared at the words and read them at least three times. Aside from the beautiful design—which first caught my attention—the words came to me as exactly what I needed to read.

The jump is so frightening between where I am and where I could be...

Because of all I may become, I will close my eyes and leap![1]

How well I understood those words. It was as if the writer had me in mind when she penned those words. I was already

---

1. Mary Ann Radmacher. Used by permission: *www.maryanneradmacher.com*

in transition and very confused. I was caught "between where I am and where I could be."

Every choice held risk—it was risky to leave my present position, it was risky to stay. If I resigned, should I leave right away or wait another year? How long did I plan before I took action?

Was I going to jump? I didn't know. Or perhaps I did, but I hadn't said yes to myself. In my case, the college had grown, we had a strong board, and finances were doing well. If I stayed, we could have continued growing and produced more of the same—more students, more money, more buildings, and more programs. I had thrived on building up Beulah Heights.

Someone had moved my ladder: It was now leaning against the wrong wall. One of the things that struck me was the difference between building an organization and running it. I had started as the former and was becoming the latter. In those early days of godly dissatisfaction, I heard myself say aloud, "I'm a builder." I knew the words were true. Running programs or institutions bores me. "It's all built. I don't care about numbers, statistics, graphs, and charts." One aspect of my work still intrigued me. That one part of my work—and it was fairly small—brightened my worst days. I functioned as a leadership consultant. "I want to help leaders reach their highest potential," I said. I want to serve leaders as their *dream releaser*. My vision is to help others succeed.

In those days, I realized that almost every pastor I met or CEO I consulted with, I was building them up, encouraging them, and helping them succeed. Dream releasing was ongoing and always new. When I met with my new client in Charlotte, for example, the experience would be new. Each consultation brightened my day.

"What does that mean?" I asked myself.

CHAPTER THREE

HANGING ON TO LADDERS

A LTHOUGH I HAD BEEN THE PRESIDENT of a college for fourteen years, I had developed a sideline of expertise. It wasn't something I planned—it just happened. When I interacted with a variety of leaders in different contexts, I became aware that I was helping them. It took me years to realize that I helped organizational leaders succeed.

Even though I wasn't aware, the more consulting I did, the more enthusiastic I became. This sideline forced me to read more books, pamphlets, Internet articles, and listen to more tapes and lectures than I ever had before. Except for my days as a college student, I couldn't remember when I had felt such a driving zeal to know more and to understand better.

Slowly—very slowly—I realized what I wanted: "I want to be a dream releaser," I said. But was I right to want to do that?

I have the capacity for self-delusion or self-deception. What if I was wrong? What if this was a mistake or a temporary dissatisfaction? What if this was a burnout situation and not truly godly dissatisfaction? What if this wasn't the ladder God wanted me to climb? It took a few weeks of internal struggle for me to become fairly confident I was moving in the right direction.

Once I had a sense of where I thought I wanted to go, my first step was to seek counsel. This is one principle I strongly advocate: Before we take any action on switching from one ladder to another, we need to seek counsel from others. Although I had vacillated, I knew it was time to move beyond my own frame of reference. I needed to talk to other leaders, who not only understood transitions, but who had also made them.

I thought of the words of Paul the apostle. He spent time alone after his conversion and preached the gospel. Apparently, he understood before most of the other disciples that God loved Gentiles (non- Jews) as much as Jews. He preached indiscriminately to anyone who would listen. Finally, just to be certain he was doing the right thing, he took a few companions and visited the church leaders. He writes that he "...communicated to them that gospel which I preach among the Gentiles, but privately to those who were of reputation, lest by any means I have run, or had run in vain" (Galatians 2:2, NKJV).

That was the point: "Lest by any means I have run, or had run in vain." In my case, I wasn't asking anyone to tell me I was running in the wrong direction. I wanted help and direction so that I could run more effectively. If this truly was God's will for me, the counsel of the wise would guide me along the right path.

Many of us aren't good at opening up to others. We feel we can handle it alone. Or we may be too ashamed to admit that we don't know how to handle our own lives.

Here are two examples of how people go about this step.

I don't know how to tell my friend Marvin that I need to talk. In fact, I wait until we're chatting over a cup of coffee and then I say casually, "You know, Marvin, I'm thinking about leaving and here's how I see the situation."

I talk; he listens. I pass on information, but I'm not asking him for input.

By contrast, I call my friend Ralph and say, "I need to talk about something, and I'd like your input." Once I sit down in his office, I say, "I'm thinking about leaving my present position for a new one. What do you think? Help me think through the issues. Ask me any question you want."

Ralph listens to my dreams. He talks; I listen carefully to the counsel I receive. Because I've told him, Ralph knows how to respond, and he's able to look at my situation far more objectively than I can.

When I don't ask for counsel, I'm passing on information; when I ask for input, I'm asking for advice. I don't invite Marvin to ask me tough questions or to push me to think differently. In fact, my conversation probably comes across as if I were saying, "This is what I'm going to do. I'm telling you what I've already made up my mind to do."

Many of us, because of our own inner insecurities, are ambivalent about opening ourselves up to anyone else. Even if we want to open up, it's not easy. When we speak with those who can help us the most, it's as if we expect them to read our minds because we can't say the words, "Help me. Help me think this thing through."

People have offered excuses for not opening up, but I'm convinced that God intended for us to share our burdens with others and the Bible affirms this. When God spoke to Peter about opening the doors of the church to Gentiles, he conferred with other leaders (see Acts 11). Kings Saul and David both sought guidance from Samuel. I also thought of another important verse: "Where there is no counsel, the people fail; but in the multitude of counselors, there is safety" (Proverbs 11:14, NKJV).

The point is that unless we open up and benefit from the wisdom of others, we're apt to make unwise decisions. I didn't want to make the mistake of not listening to those with a different perspective. Once I made the decision to seek counsel, my first questions were: Whom do I ask? Who will be the most helpful? Talking to the wrong people could frustrate or discourage me. I needed to focus on those who had the experience and expertise to offer insight.

To prepare for sharing my situation, I sat at my desk and made a profile of the people I wanted to talk to about leaving Beulah Heights. Because I wanted totally objective responses, I decided to eliminate anyone who would be involved in or affected by my decision.

I want to make it clear that my wife Brenda would be the most adversely affected if things went wrong. But we believed in the biblical concept that a husband and a wife become one (Genesis 2:24; Matthew 19:6). She functioned not only as part of me but as my sounding board throughout the whole process. I talked with her about some of the inner issues that I was not able to talk about with others.

- This isn't my complete list, but here are the major factors:
- They had to be Christians. I wanted leaders who had the same foundational values as I do.
- They needed to be on the high end of leadership—achievers themselves.
- They had to be leaders who had left one organization and moved on to another or started a new one.
- They would not be pastors who had moved from one church to another. (Moving from one church to another is a transition, but still within the same essential situation.)
- They had to be people engaged in fields totally different from mine. While that was a major transition, I was going to be moving to another field. I needed an outside-the-box perspective.

We don't go around and ask advice of anyone who will listen to us. We need to be selective about whom we ask. I had decided to talk only to those who could give me *professional* advice.

After I decided on the type of people I wanted to consult, I made my list—adding and subtracting names until I knew I had the people with whom I could talk freely. I ended up with fourteen names. One by one, I called and made appointments to spend time with them when they could carefully advise me.

I was going to climb a ladder I had never climbed before. I didn't know if it was securely planted or how high it would reach. Was I scared? Yes, I was. But I was also scared not to take the risk. Because I wanted to be sure I was taking the right risk, I asked other risk-takers for guidance.

I wasn't asking any of them to offer the traditional advice we get from the cautious or timid:

- "I think you ought to pray more about this."
- "Don't you think you've got a good thing going now?"
- "Why leave now? Enjoy the fruit of your labors."
- "A lot of people get great ideas but they don't work out."

Although I had more than fourteen names on my original list, I didn't talk to all of them. By the time I had gone down the first half of my list, I also realized I had received the guidance I needed.

The reason I didn't speak to all of those on my original list was that, even though they had good hearts, a few of them were stabilizers. They were good people and I liked them, but I wasn't looking for stability; I wanted effectiveness. Too often, stability can get in the way. Consistency can thwart progress. I could go anywhere and be consistent.

MY COUNSELORS

My wife **Brenda** was my sounding board throughout the whole thing. I talked with her about some inner issues that I was not able to talk about with others. If my decisions were bad, she would be the one most adversely affected.

Dr. Garnet Pike, Dean of Southwestern Christian University in Bethany, Oklahoma, is a great leader. He heads up their leadership department. He has been through some major transitions himself and was able to give me some wonderful advice.

Dr. Crawford Loritts is Associate Director of Campus Crusade, and a prolific author. He has a daily radio program on the Moody network and has become a great friend. He helped me think through the pragmatic issues as well as some integrity issues.

Calvin Edwards is one of the most strategic thinkers I know. He is Founder & CEO of the Calvin Edwards & Company. His organization advises philanthropists how to give money wisely. He has been involved with many different Christian organizations. Because he has made major transitions, he was able to help me think through some of the issues of control and independence.

My friend **Don Chapman** is the Chairman of the Atlanta Metropolitan Foundation. He is also on the boards of AirTran Airlines and Longhorn Steakhouse. He kept saying, "When you leave, leave."

William "Billy" Mitchell is Chairman of Carter & Associates, one of the largest commercial development firms in downtown Atlanta. He is a great friend and a strategic thinker. At the time I went to him, Billy had just gone through a transition from CEO to becoming Chairman of the company. He was able to teach me some of the things that he did well and things he wished he had done differently.

Pastor Roger Brumlow, is District Superintendent of the Assemblies of God for the state of Georgia. He had moved from a church setting to an ecclesiastical, denominational position. That's a major transition and he was able to help me think through some of the issues.

Dr. John Maxwell left a large church in San Diego and moved to Atlanta to start his own company (INJOY), and he has been successful. John had taken a large risk—and in some ways, my risk would be just as great. Like him, I was moving away from security and certainty.

Dr. John Hull is president of EQUIP, the nonprofit ministry of John Maxwell. Before he joined EQUIP, he was a Toronto pastor. John helped me relate my move to the transitions that he went through.

Dr. Jim Flanagan, President of Luther Rice Seminary, used to be the dean and has become the most successful president the college has had. However, there is a big difference. Even though it's the same institution, the transition is enormous from dean to president. He had moved from the area of academia to the role of president—and a large part of that job is fundraising. Because I thought the board might want me to become chancellor, I knew his experiences could be helpful.

Apostle Lafayette Scales, Columbus, Ohio, Rhema Christian Center, is a great leader. He has led churches, as well as other nonprofit organizations, and sits on many different boards. He asked me tough questions that I needed to answer. I don't think I would have answered them without someone else prodding me.

Kevin Miller, who is a great entrepreneur and philanthropist, has lived most of his professional life in transition because he starts companies and then sells them. He also buys troubled companies, fixes them, and helps them become profitable. God has blessed him to grasp transitions from outside the church-world perspective but always with a human touch.

Dr. Bob Lupton is President of Family Counseling Services/ Urban Ministries in Atlanta. He not only has gone through transitions himself but he has helped many other people go through transitions. Therefore, he was able to help me think through the nonprofit issues, staffing, and working with the board.

So these are the fourteen people who helped me in making my decision. One thing that stands out to me in retrospect is that not one of the individuals I spoke to cautioned me against leaving. Perhaps because they're all entrepreneurs at heart, they know the thrill of risk taking. All of them had moved from security to embrace challenges.

They sensed I was moving in the right direction and at the right time. In consulting with those on my list, none of them challenged me to stay and make Beulah Heights larger. By then, I was so far along in the process, I wasn't positive where I was going to end up, but I had to move from my comfortable ladder. I was convinced I couldn't remain the president of a Bible college much longer.

• • •

The best piece of advice from each of them was, "Go for it." Don Chapman said one thing that I still remember vividly: "And when you walk away, walk away. Don't look back." "Don't second guess yourself," John Maxwell said. "You've been struggling with this, so do what you need to do. You can't reach second base if you're keeping one foot on first."

I had listened to all kinds of pro and con arguments inside my head. Many nights I lay in the darkness playing out the worst scenario and the best. I tried to see every possible angle. When I opened up to people like John Maxwell and Don Chapman, none of them asked me a question that I had not already wrestled with.

Just knowing I had wrestled with all the issues confirmed to me that I had done the right thing. I went to them because I needed outside people for perspective. The greatest need of a high-end leader is perspective. Good, helpful consultants offer us perspective—they help us see things in a different light. They ask the same questions we've already thought about—or should have.

To answer myself was one thing, but when someone I trust asks a question, stares at me, and waits, I'll probably answer differently. I can lie to myself or convince myself of something I want to believe, but when someone else asks me, I'm more apt to get gut-level honest.

• • •

As I pondered the question of leaving, one central question kept hitting me: *Is this the right time to change ladders?* That's a big issue and the area where many leaders mess up.

They leave too early.

They leave before they've set everything in place.

They leave too late.

Don't we all know of organizations and churches where the leader has held on to the power and has refused to let go? The organization could have run smoother and perhaps moved in new and more challenging directions, but the person in charge couldn't step back.

Three years before I resigned, I became aware of my need for transition, but I couldn't do it then. I hadn't prepared for the takeover. Four things were going on that made it impossible for me to step aside at that time.

The college was going through accreditation renewal.

We were going through federal financial aid re-approval.

The board had not aligned itself. It was a good board, but the chemistry wasn't quite right. I knew that it would take another year or two of working together and building trust before we had the kind of synergy we needed.

Dr. Benson Karanja wasn't ready.

I knew all along that Dr. Benson Karanja should be my successor, but he still needed another year-and-a-half to two years to fit into the position. Part of his fitting in was to introduce him to things I did and make him part of the transactions I went through. People needed to know him and to trust him. I sent him in my place to meetings and made him more accountable. I never told him what I had planned for him. If he complained (he never did), I would have known I was mistaken, and that he wasn't the man for the job.

I had to make sure the timing was right for the transition to take place.

Then came decision time.

On Easter Sunday, 2003, my wife and I had been to Columbus, Georgia, where I preached at Solid Rock church. We were driving back to the south side of Atlanta where we live. We spoke about the situation of my resigning—and those minutes together turned into a powerful experience that is forever etched in my mind.

What made the conversation surprising was that Brenda and I had talked—in fact, I thought we had talked the issue to death and there was nothing else to say. Together we had looked at the transition from every possible angle. "What if this doesn't happen?" "What if that happens?" We figured on expenses and made budgets. We made what we called a fact budget and also a faith budget. I had learned long ago that God's numbers were always bigger than mine, so I wanted to think on two different levels.

Crawford Lorrits, one of my fourteen mentors, taught me about a business plan and used the acronym of DOCTOR.

D = Directional

O = Objectives

C = Cash

T = Tracking

O = Overall Evaluation

R = Refinements.

It's a good way for me to focus my thinking and find concrete ways to start fleshing out my thinking, and I started writing more.

For example *Cash* refers to the whole business, the overall picture: What do I see myself doing at the end of the day? How am I going to make adjustments? What's really my objective?

I assumed there was a good way to do a business plan. I wrote portions of such a plan, but not all of it. For example, I didn't write anything under Refinements; I'm not there yet. Cash, I sat down with my financial planner Bill Youngblood and went through the whole thing. We had already called a meeting with him, our CPA, Brenda, and me, and we planned the whole thing.

That Sunday afternoon as we drove north on I-185, Brenda was quiet for a few seconds, then she said. "Let's go for it."

Just those words.

They were enough.

They rang like giant bells inside my heart. I knew it was right. And we made the decision right then—together.

In the summer of 2004, I went on a fishing trip to Missoula, Montana, with a group of six men. We sat inside a flatbed metal boat and drifted down the Bitter Root River for eight hours. We didn't worry about direction. After all, when we drift there is only one way to go—the way the current pulls. That was fine—we planned to drift.

That's probably one of the few times I've enjoyed drifting. I'm action oriented and I like to see things happening. One day when I was still at Beulah Heights, I admitted to myself that I was drifting. Things were going on, but I wasn't making them happen. They were happening because I had set things in action in the months and years before.

The first awareness of drifting took place five years before I left.

For at least two years, I lived in denial.

To explain, it's helpful for me to use the ladder image, I had climbed high. One day I awakened to the fact that I had stopped climbing. I was holding on, staring at the view, no longer interested in ascending farther. Perhaps I was high enough so that others couldn't see that I wasn't moving. Or perhaps I had set up so much action below me, no one had time to think about my movement and me. No one saw that I wasn't moving, *but I knew*. For me, it isn't enough to stare at the distance I had covered or the rungs I had climbed and smile at the level of success I enjoyed.

That was a new place for me—somewhere I had never been before. It was also the first time I didn't feel the challenge—the push—to take the next step upward on the ladder.

If I had faced that impasse as a pastor, my thinking would have been something like this: "It will soon be Sunday again and we'll have a nice church service. The Sunday after that we'll be doing the same thing." This was the step beyond the godly dissatisfaction.

People at the school continued to speak of growth—and our student population still increased. Everything moved along nicely. That was part of the dissatisfaction. Why wouldn't the school move forward? I had set in motion several programs that still brought in results. The momentum would carry us for another year or two, but I wasn't stepping up to the next rung, and, of course, there were more rungs to climb.

We were already doing things no other school was doing. For example, we had a degree program in Portuguese because we have a large Brazilian population in Atlanta and we had contracted with former, well-educated missionaries to teach them. We had started holding classes early in the mornings so students could go to college before they went to their jobs. We held extension classes all over Metro Atlanta.

I'm sure there were other things we could have done, but I wasn't doing new things. I was standing on the same rung. I had a difficult time saying to myself, "Sam, you're not going anywhere. You're standing exactly where you stood three months ago or five months ago." Admitting to myself that life isn't going anywhere was difficult—especially when people kept praising me for the good things they saw happening.

Our budget had increased, enrollment zoomed upward, and financial support was high. No matter which direction I looked, the school was progressing. "The school isn't the problem," I said to myself. "Sam Chand is the problem." We leaders have a hard time admitting such things to ourselves. We don't see ourselves drifting with the current or just standing still. We tell ourselves that we're tired, burned out, or we need to get away for a re-charge, but we don't stand still! Not us. We're visionaries and we're going somewhere. Sometimes, however, we mistake motion for action. We see activity and call it progress. Sometimes our vision is self-delusional.

One day I finally admitted a significant fact: *If I'm not leading, I'm drifting.*

How many leaders will say that? I did, but only after a difficult, self-searching period. I asked myself questions about being fulfilled. Do I still find joy in this job? Am I growing as a person? as a professional? as a leader? Do I love coming to work every morning?

One of my friends, who had just started his twenty-first year in his present position, said, "Almost every morning I wake up and thank God that I'm getting paid for doing work that I love. I talk to so many people who hate what they're doing. When I hear that, I'm even more aware how truly blessed I am."

I knew that feeling, and I had felt that way for years after I became president of Beulah Heights, but I wasn't feeling that excitement. I had stopped climbing.

At the same time, I increasingly received invitations to counsel pastors of large congregations. I had to stay sharp for that—they were outstanding leaders and people of vision—so I read, thought, and searched for answers. I was growing in that area, but I wasn't growing in the job I was being paid to do.

Again, I refer to my co-writer, who had been a pastor for fourteen years before he became a full-time writer. He had begun to write as a creative sideline. "One day I had an identity crisis," he said. "I had to decide if I was a preacher who wrote or a writer who preached." He struggled with that question for several months. He said that, as far as he could tell, no one in his congregation suspected the dilemma. The membership continued to grow and the offerings had not dipped, but *he knew*. Eventually, he switched ladders.

When he first became pastor of the church, he told the board that one day he might want to write full time. "If my writing ever becomes more important than being a pastor," he said, "I'll know it six months before you do. I'll resign before you're aware of what's going on."

That's exactly what happened: Every member of the board expressed surprise; no one had suspected anything.

Like my co-writer, I needed to make a change, but I didn't admit it to myself for nearly two years. The tension slowly built. Finally, I asked: Can I continue to urge others to keep climbing if I've stopped on the fifteenth rung? How could I lead others where I haven't gone? My first indications came with that inner dissatisfaction, but it was deeper. It was internal and nothing showed externally.

As I look back, I realize that I went through five stages in my transition.

FIVE STAGES OF TRANSITION

Stage 1—Pre-contemplation

Stage 2—Contemplation

Stage 3—Darkness

Stage 4—Insight

Stage 5—Action

The only way I can explain it is to call the first step *pre-contemplation*. Pre-contemplation goes on when we know something ought to happen, but we don't know what. Something's not right, but we can't figure it out. This means we look at ourselves and wonder why we've failed or why we're not as committed to God or to our jobs as we used to be. The second stage is *contemplation*. This is the stage of awareness. We know these facts:

I'm not lazy.

I'm not losing out with God.

I'm not running away.

We're not taking action, but we become aware that something will have to change.

Stage three is *darkness*. This is the most difficult place. I can't see to climb the next rung; I don't know how to go backward in all of the darkness. I knew I didn't want to be where I'd been but I honestly didn't know where I wanted to go. We finally ask ourselves, "What do I do now?"

Even those who have an inkling of where they want to go next seem to have to go through the darkness. They catch a glimpse of what can be but they don't see how it can come about.

"I can't go backward and I don't know where forward is," I said. "It's not neutral; it's drifting." This is a stage of inner confusion. I was growing increasingly aware of the need for change, but I didn't know what to do or how to take the next step.

I called it a funk. The word comes from the name of Casmir Funk, a Polish biochemist who used his name to refer to dietary deficiencies. It has come to refer to someone in a pessimistic state, someone who is unable to engage actively.

I didn't know where to go because I didn't know what to do. I didn't know how to go forward and I wasn't ready to step backward. It's a terrible place—and *terrible* is the best word I can think of. Once we know where we want to go, we can face the challenge. We can take action.

Particularly as Christians, we groan and agonize as we cry out to God, "What is your will?" We truly want to know. We keep saying, "Show me what to do and I'll do it." We also seek explanations or assurances.

I wasn't ready to fulfill the message of the greeting card: I will close my eyes and leap! I didn't know how to leap. I knew the leap would come—once I had a sense of direction again.

I didn't know who I was then. I knew who I had been, and always thought I knew where I was going. I felt different, and it was as if the rules of the game have changed and no one has explained them to me. I wanted to move (remember, I'm action oriented) but with no sense of direction, what could I do? Do I step down a rung? Move up one rung or two? In many ways, this isn't the most crucial stage, but it's the most difficult because we have no sense of direction. All we know is that we don't want to be where we are now.

Stage four is *insight*. This can happen in an instant or it can be like the first rays of light in the morning—they slowly push away the darkness. Sometimes it's knowing what to do without knowing how we know. It's as if the Holy Spirit whispers, "This is the way, walk in it." That also indicates that it's a way we've never been before.

Even with the insight, doubts may creep in. As soon as we get the insight, we argue with ourselves. "Can this be right?" "What if...?"

We don't want to stay on the same ladder, but we don't know which ladder to climb. Pastors are a prime candidate for such trauma. They know they are no longer being effective, and going to another church is torture for them. Or they may be effective but they've lost the heart for what they're doing where they are. Or they achieve success and it feels empty because the thrill of growth has gone. They don't know what to do next because that's what they've been trained to do. If they ask trusted friends, they'll usually get the answer that another church is probably the response. It may be just that: a new challenge or a new ladder to climb. But it may be that another church would feel exactly like the same ladder they've already been climbing. The higher up the ladder we climb, the more confusing it is to us.

Or to use the image of climbing a mountain, we think we'll reach the summit—and we do—but then we see other mountains and they beckon to us. They're higher mountains and we realize that's where we want to go. As I stared at the various mountains, I thought, they're not bad mountains, they're great mountains, but they weren't *my* mountains.

This is also harder for people who can do many things. I had many job offers—and I never went out looking for any of them. One job offer was to become an administrator of a huge church; they would start me off at a high six-figure income a year—more money than I've ever made in my life. It didn't even sound good.

As I continued to listen to God, I didn't know which ladder I was to switch to, I knew only two things.

First, I was going to leave this ladder.

Second, for several months, when I examined a new ladder, it wasn't the right one for me. In my case, it was an elimination process. That's exactly what happened in my life. No, that's not for me, I'd think. No, that won't be long term. Questions also popped out, such as, "Will I do this for the rest of my life?" "If this is the last job I ever have, will I enjoy it?"

To use a different image, I saw bridges ahead. I'd lift my foot to step on one and see the other side. I'd shake my head. "No, not that one either." I kept moving along, scrutinizing every bridge. Some would take me across to the other side—but it wasn't the place I wanted to be.

I wasn't sure I knew where the other side was. I couldn't validate it in terms of concrete answers, but somehow I knew this is the right thing.

In my moment of insight, I realized I wanted to be a consultant to pastors and leaders in large organizations. That was a risky decision. One of my first concerns was that I would be giving up a steady income. For many years, I had been able to count on a paycheck the first of the month.

Most people don't talk about transitions; it's as if they are employed at one organization today and the next we know they're part of another. They were at one church Sunday and the following Sunday they're at a different one. It doesn't work that way—there are many things that go on.

This is where I distinguish between change and transition. Change takes place when we move one person from Department A to Department B. That involves the hard side of leadership. The soft side of leadership is all the transitional issues. Transitions may not be the word everyone likes to use. We could just as easily refer to inner wrestlings, inner turmoil, or internal confusion.

The insight persists and leads us to the fifth stage. This is the place of action. This is where we hold the gun and pull the trigger. I climb down my ladder, my feet hit the ground, and I turn my back on the old ladder. I have to do that to be ready to climb a new one.

CHAPTER FOUR
LEAVING OLD LADDERS

MAKING THE COMMITMENT to switch ladders is only the beginning—a big beginning. This sets up the procedure for the next steps we need to take.

Once Brenda and I had made the decision for me to leave my position, we had to answer this question: Once we have decided to switch ladders, whom do we tell and in what order do we tell them? For us, our children came first. Although we made our decision in April, we didn't tell them until Mother's Day, nearly a month later.

After our children, I met with Dr. Oliver Haney, Chairman of the Board at Beulah Heights Bible College. Dr. Haney was supportive, but did urge me to reconsider—if not the decision at least the timing of it. The next person on my list was the man I had been developing to replace me, Dr. Benson Karanja, Executive Vice President. I talked to Dr. Karanja in May and told him about my leaving, but he didn't know I had him in mind as the new president.

Number three on my list, Dr. James Keiller, was the hardest to tell. In talking to others who have switched ladders, they all seemed to have one or two people to whom they owed a great deal. They also knew their decision would deeply hurt or disappoint those special individuals.

Dr. Keiller had been the dean of the college when I came from India as a student in 1973. He had been a great teacher, mentor, confidant, and friend. Dr. Keiller had greatly encouraged me to become president.

At the suggestion of Dr. Tom Grinder, Dr. Keiller helped to make my position possible. Dr. Grinder, then General Overseer of our denomination, was the major catalyst and was Chairman of the Board of Beulah Heights Bible College. He was also my former pastor and a good friend. Dr. Grinder had recognized gifts in me and encouraged me. Dr. Keiller remained as Dean and VP. He applauded everything I did, and we worked together so harmoniously, he expected me to stay there until I retired. (I had assumed the same thing.)

I knew telling Dr. Keiller about my decision would hurt him, and I was afraid he would feel I had let him down. That wasn't easy for me to say or for him to hear. It was a tearful time—for both of us.

My next step was to go to the members of the board, and I wanted to do that individually. I chose to travel across the country to discuss my decision face to face with all the board members. One, I needed to personalize the process (what I call the soft side of leadership); two, issues are viewed differently one on one than in a group setting (the hard side of leadership). I wanted to maintain organizational health by inviting open dialogue.

"I've decided to resign as president," I said, "and I want you to hear it from me personally." I asked the board to act on my formal resignation at their meeting on October 14, 2003. In my mind, leaving was already an accomplished reality. They must have perceived that determination, because none of them challenged me to stay. Individually they gave me their blessing and said they would accept my resignation—reluctantly.

The board agreed. Now everything was laid out, although I asked each person not to say anything until I made a public announcement. The day after the board meeting, October 15, I called a staff meeting.

Here's one important caution for those of us who decide to switch ladders: We don't leave badly. We don't want to make enemies or hurt feelings when we leave.

Here's another bit of advice: We need to leave a door open so that we can go back. You don't plan to go back, but you never know if you'll need something from them in the future.

I never expected to return, but I have no way of knowing the future. What if I were mistaken? What if, two years later, I wanted to have some kind of association with them? Or what if I wanted to use their facilities for meetings? Or if I needed recommendations from them.

Too many resign and they're carrying bad feelings toward others. They use those last days as opportunities to vent their anger or dissatisfaction. I offer one word of advice: *Don't.*

If there are issues, we need to resolve them first or hold them until we're gone. That also means that the resignation letter needs to be thought through carefully with no venting. This is just as true regarding any public speaking opportunity. We need to leave with a smile on our face.

We don't want to react to what is wrong where we are; rather we need to focus on what is right. I'm an optimistic person and yet I found myself finding more fault in the last three or four months than I had in my fourteen years combined. I had to ask myself why that was going on.

I was disengaging. Perhaps we may need to see some of those things to help convince ourselves that we've made the right decision. Or perhaps there have been little things that we've tolerated. Now that we're disengaging, we become aware of them. We need to remind ourselves: I am not resigning because something is wrong. I am taking the next step in my life and career.

We need to keep our perspective so that even though we can see things that may need changing, they are not our reason for leaving.

•••

I wrote a letter of resignation that went first to the board of trustees and then to our general constituency. This is the first paragraph:

The last fourteen years have been my best in every way. I have no regret. I began serving BHBC as president on July 1, 1989. Who would have thought, in 1973 when "student" Samuel Chand was serving BHBC as janitor, cook, and dishwasher that I would return as "president" of the same college! Some say, "Only in America..." I say, "Only with God!"

I followed with a grid of achievements the school had made in the fourteen years. For example, we had 20,000 volumes in our library, and that number had reached 43,000. We had no federal financial aid, and now BHBC could receive full benefits. Our annual budget had grown from $200,000 to $3,400,000.

Too often, CEOs and pastors leave and they decide that as long as they're leaving, they will take their parting shots at everyone. Instead of facing the individuals with whom they had difficulties, they take the passive/aggressive pathway and vent grievances before everyone.

In my case, there was nothing to vent about, because I had been treated well, loved the people I worked with, and felt an immense amount of gratitude to God for the years I had been the president.

One pastor actually said in his final sermon: "As a congregation, we could have been much farther down the road had God's people chosen to follow Him." He was the same man who couldn't understand why the church members didn't love him.

When we leave, leave. We make it clean, neat, and quick.

There's nothing more we can do. If we vent, we're only letting out our aggression. Isn't that a cowardly way of leaving a situation?

When we leave, we want to have a genuine smile on our face, warmth in our heart, and hear no angry noises behind us.

In my case, I didn't want anyone to think I was jumping off a sinking ship or that I had some information that we were in decline. More than once, I made it clear that nothing was wrong, I wasn't going to a rival school, and I had no dissatisfactions. I wasn't trying to say that life was perfect, but my relationship with everyone—so far as I knew—had been excellent.

Two things we don't say: First, "I've taken you as far as I can." That would not have been true for me. If I had stayed, I could have helped Beulah Heights continue to grow, but I wouldn't have done it with the enthusiasm I felt in 1989 or even 2002.

The second thing we don't say is, "God is finished with me here." That also wasn't true—I didn't believe God was finished; I did feel Sam Chand was finished. I felt that as long as I stayed, God would always have something for me to do. But Beulah Heights wasn't where I could be the most effective in the kingdom of God.

I had grown during my years at the head of the college. I had come as a student in the fall of 1973. Twelve years after graduating, I came back as the president. They were wonderful years, yet we faced many problems. In the early days, we wondered if we should close the school.

Enrollment was low.

Finances were low as well.

The small staff was overwhelmed.

Buildings needed repairs.

Morale needed boosting.

I acknowledged those needs but chose to consider them challenges and learning experiences. The board totally backed me.

My years as the head of the school also enabled me to have the kind of public platform I have today. Had I remained the pastor of a congregation, I would have had a ministry, but not nearly as wide as the one God gave me through my association with Beulah Heights. They were wonderful, exciting years, but it was time to bring them to a close. I had to leave because God had new doors waiting for me to open and walk through.

•••

There is something else I want to point out about resigning from any organization.

Our exit strategy is more important than our entrance. That is, how we leave is more important than how we came in. When CEOs or pastors discuss leaving with me, I ask, "What will you be remembered for?"

I tell them about my resigning from Beulah Heights. When I became president in 1989, we had only 87 students. When I left on December 31, 2003, we had 690. The point, however, is that none of the students from 1989 were still there. None of those students who welcomed me would be there when I left. So I asked, "How would I be remembered? How did I want to be remembered?"

The answer seemed obvious: I want to be remembered for how I left rather than how I came in. We can all tell stories of leaders who came in to change things and everyone rallied behind them. They used words such as "greatest" or "biggest" or "most spiritual," but they didn't last. As the old saying goes, "They came in with a roar and went out with a whimper."

I think people spend too much time on how they're going to go into a place. That's important, of course, but how we leave is going to follow us. People remember our departure, and they tell others. Many pastors left good churches, and CEOs left good organizations, but they departed in such a way that their reception at the next place was tainted. Word does get around.

We must never forget that we live in a very small world. People talk to people. News has a way of traveling. Wherever we land next, information about how we left the previous place follows. This is especially true if the new employer starts a background check.

Here is one true story my co-writer tells. His friend, whom I'll call Michael, was the pastor of a struggling church in Metro Atlanta. After eight years, Michael resigned to become pastor of another church. He called his final sermon, "What We Did Wrong." That title should have alerted everyone. For the next forty minutes, he went down a long list of grievances—mainly the way the congregation had failed him. Not once did he ever admit he had failed.

A week after Michael arrived at his new church, the head elder showed him a copy of a letter that a member of his previous church had written to the board. It had about a hundred signatures at the bottom. They listed fourteen ways Michael had failed them and urged the new board either "to watch him closely or get rid of him before he does serious harm."

Michael convinced the board that the people who wrote were disgruntled, unspiritual, didn't want to follow God, and had hindered every program he tried.

Nineteen months later, the church asked for Michael's resignation. Too late, the board of the church realized they should have followed through and checked up on the list of grievances.

When any leader leaves and parts with harsh words, bitterness, fractured relationships, or in a passive-aggressive manner, there is nothing to celebrate. If there is celebration for their leaving at a farewell, it's either perfunctory or a sense of, "At least he's leaving."

Here's another true story. One businessman told me he was going to leave in three months but hadn't made it known. He told me all the admonishments he was going to deliver. "I want them to re-think everything and make it easier for the person who follows me." He asked my opinion about the things he was going to say.

Although I knew he wanted me to rally behind him, I said, "Sounds stupid to me."

A startled look appeared on his face.

"You're leaving. You can't do anything, so why do you want to hurt people? The only person you hurt is yourself. Just think about the reaction of those who will have heard of your dissatisfaction. They'll say or at least think, 'If that's how he felt about us, why did he stay so long?'"

In this instance, the man listened. I also urged him to make peace with everyone in the organization with whom he had any problems.

When my co-writer resigned his church to become a full-time writer, there was one elder in the congregation with whom he had never been able to resolve differences. The man would always smile and say, "Everything's fine," but word filtered back how un-fine things were. That same elder didn't attend services the last two weeks. When Cec Murphey phoned, he got a voice message and the man didn't return his call. The day after he left, Cec wrote the elder a letter with these words: "I'm sorry we didn't have a good working relationship. I don't know how I failed you or where I went wrong, but I am sorry. Please forgive me for anything I've done wrong."

Cec didn't want to imply fault or accuse the elder of anything. The elder never replied—and Cec hadn't expected a response. Ten years later, Cec assisted the current minister of that church in a funeral. Afterward, one of the older members referred to the troublesome elder, who had since moved out of the city. "He showed me the letter you wrote. You did the right thing."

That's how we need to leave any position: to do everything we can to make peace and to mend bad relationships—as much as it depends on us. Thus, how we leave is more critical than how we arrive.

All of this is to say, we need to think through our exit strategy carefully.

• • •

As I've mentioned previously, no one at Beulah Heights realized it, but I had been working on the exit strategy for three years. I went about it methodically. I wanted the school to succeed after my departure, so I surreptitiously set up a succession plan. I wanted to leave with credibility. I also wanted to make sure the school was in good financial shape. When I left, I assumed some of our supporters might want to stop giving to the school. I began to prepare Dr. Karanja, but I didn't say a word to him. I wanted him to grow naturally into the job and eliminate any pressure about whether he would fail or succeed. I learned to disengage myself slowly. Part of that came through delegating. I worked hard to empower others. I devoted a lot of energy to developing leadership in others on the staff.

My most difficult task in leaving, however, and I assume this is true of all leaders, is to give up control. Once leaders say, "I'm leaving," power and control are out of their hands. They can't determine the future or the decisions others will make. I did the best I could.

I learned something about leaving from my co-writer. When he left the pastorate, in his final sermon (and again later at the church's reception), he said, "I've tried to serve you faithfully while I've been here. I've loved you and have wanted only the best for you. I'm leaving, and I want you to transfer your loyalty and love to the person who replaces me."

He didn't point out that he had succeeded a pastor who had been there for seventeen years. The former pastor occasionally visited church members and agreed to conduct funerals. He would consent to officiate at weddings and instruct the couple to call the church office to make sure the space was available. Not once did he ever contact the current pastor.

Even though the man had chosen to resign and had become pastor of a church nearly an hour's drive away, either he didn't want to give up control or refused to relinquish his authority. (Those he counseled became increasingly marginal in leadership and posed little threat.)

Cec Murphey didn't want his successor to go through such experiences. "Please don't call me or write to me. It's not lack of love on my part, and I think you know that. I want you to remember me as someone who used to be available to you."

Only one member called him and he told her to call the interim pastor. "But he doesn't know me like you do," she said.

"Then give him the chance to know you."

• • •

Someone went before me; someone will come after me. I can serve with my utmost commitment where I am right now; I can also look ahead and prepare the rungs for my successor to climb.

Not everyone can focus on the future. Some are too insecure and not even sure they can stay on the ladder themselves, but wise, secure leaders plan for their succession the day they start the job. We often say that a baby starts dying the day it is born. We can do great service for our organization if we start the process early. We can't always pick our successors, but we can prepare for them. I couldn't pick my successor, but I could—and did—create a healthy environment and climate in which healthy conversations could take place. No matter what our leadership role, we can begin to shape the profile of the next person to follow.

Here's how it worked out for me. Although I prepared for three years, my board asked me to remain as chancellor for the next two years—really the same thing as an ambassador at large. I have no office, no staff, and absolutely no authority.

The board understood my name was important to be associated with the college while my successor moved into his position. *In a healthy environment, no one feels threatened.* They understood that connectivity was part of the life of the organization and they saw value in it. I created a healthy place where they could see the benefits of my name remaining part of the school. They asked me to allow my name to remain attached because of issues of accreditation, finances, and donors. "Until Dr. Karanja comes into his own, can you remain part of the phase-out plan?"

Of course I could—and I hadn't expected that kind of generosity.

●●●

I looked ahead to ask what problems my departure could cause Dr. Karanja. One of the things had to do with several staff people who needed to be released. They had been with me for a long time, and I could handle them. I wanted to make sure that my successor wouldn't have to deal with my unfinished business. They weren't the best, and the longer they stayed and the more complex our systems became, the less effectively they did their jobs. I wanted to make sure that my successor wouldn't have any dead wood to deal with. I let a few people go—and that wasn't easy—but it was the right thing to do.

What issues do I need to deal with while I still can do something about them? John Maxwell gave me this advice. "In the last few months, ask yourself, what can I do now that will help the next man?"

He said that he cleaned house. There were people who needed to go. He didn't want his successor to have his problems because he's the one who hired those people. I did that for Dr. Karanja in great part. I called in a few trusted staff people and asked them in confidence, "Who do you want to see leave? Who isn't carrying a full load or isn't fitting in?" They gave me names—and all of them gave the same names. I released those who weren't carrying their loads. It wasn't easy, but I believe I did the right thing.

• • •

I also had to deal with communications from well-meaning people who questioned my decision in spiritual terms. I started getting notes from one of my major donors. This was one of them:

"There is the perfect will of God and there is the permissive will of God," he wrote. "I don't believe what you're planning is the perfect will of God. Brother Sam, the best place to be is in the perfect will of God."

How did I answer such a statement? I saw it as his concern and compassion for me. If I tried to answer, I assumed he would rush back with a reason why I was mistaken.

I chose not to respond. There was no sense in having that conversation. He wouldn't change my mind; I knew I couldn't change his. There was nowhere for me to go on that one, so I just left it alone.

CHAPTER FIVE
LIFE PURPOSES

W HO AM I? Everyone asks that question (or should) somewhere in life—and it's an important issue to grapple with. A second question, not asked as often, follows: What is my life purpose?

Years ago, I first asked myself that question and stayed with it until I had an answer. I could have asked it in many ways:

- What is my life purpose?
- What am I gifted to do?
- What are my greatest abilities and how do I use them?
- What produces the best results?
- Where do I find the greatest fulfillment?

Instead, I focused on the question about life purpose: What do I do best? When and how am I the most effective in my life? I didn't have any magic moment or instant stroke of enlightenment, but I gradually came to realize that *I'm a dream releaser*. I love to help others succeed. Others have dreams but don't seem to know how to make those dreams turn into reality. God has given me the ability to help them release those dreams.

That pushed me to ask, "Okay, how do I know if I'm being effective at releasing others' dreams?" I looked at what I had already accomplished at Beulah Heights. My ideas had worked and we had developed a great school—not perfect but good. We had come a long way in the years I had been there.

What is God doing in my life? I asked. What are my gifts? What is being affirmed most by me? Where do I find the greatest fulfillment?

The question doesn't stop there—it's something we must continue to push and probe. Once I answered one question, another popped up and then another.

Wise leaders explore the soft side of themselves—and we all have a soft side as well as a hard side. The hard side refers to getting the business done and making objective decisions. I also needed to move beyond the objective and look at my subjective side. For a long time, I had majored in the hard side. I thought of that part as the tough decisions we make when we rely on outward criteria, examine the facts, analyze situations, and make choices on an impersonal level. Good leaders do that fairly well.

Sometimes those good leaders could become *great* leaders if they would open up their soft side. My co-writer refers to two kinds of writers—and this is just as true of leaders in any area. They are either cool, objective or warm, subjective. Most writers, he says, can do both, but they have a preference.

I had worked hard to build up my hard side and I realized I also need to work as diligently to explore and develop the warm, subjective side.

What makes me pound the table with passion? What makes me weep? What brings me joy? What kind of interactions enable me to walk away saying to myself, "Yes! Yes. I have a sense of fulfillment"?

The soft side is the part that affirms someone, that pats a worker on the back and says, "That was a great response."

It's as simple as my saying to Dr. Karanja after a business meeting (which I did more than once), "Thank you for pulling us back to the issue. We kept trying to stray, but you wouldn't let us. That was good and I appreciate your doing that."

As the two sides of my self slowly merged, I saw the distinction this way: The hard side of leadership knows what we need to do, how, and when. This part revolves around principles. The soft side comes out of values and interpersonal responses. Whom will this decision involve? Who will be affected? What's going to be the transitional issue?

For example, let's see how this works in change and transition. Change is the hard fact. I move a lamp from one side of the room to another. That is change. Transition, however, asks, "Is the electrical cord long enough to reach?" In the church, I can change the worship leader, or in a corporation, I can change the manager of production, but whom will my actions affect? That's the soft side. The timing of it is the soft side. It takes into account the big picture of all that is involved.

It's principle contrasted with people. Only a fraction of good, strong, leadership is the hard side. (Yet that's where most of the leadership books focus.) What ruins programs and hurts people comes from the soft side of leadership. Some people are most comfortable dealing with systems, numbers, and facts. They're the ones who expend enormous effort on organizational charts and rules. Those things aren't wrong, *but it's the attitude that lies behind the action.* They tend to move a person from one position to another as a way to solve the problem. All they've done is move the problem from the third floor to the sixth.

It's like saying, "You are going to have cancer in your shoulder. Do you want it on the right side or the left?" Think of the male choir member who causes problems. "Why don't we get him out of the choir and involved in the men's ministry?" That solves the problem for the choir, but what does it do to the men's ministry?

I see the soft side operating in many ways. One of them is in casual conversation. That's the intuitive part of us at work. Soft leadership can also ruin us; hard facts are so easy to adhere to, anyone can figure out the hard side—although they are not always able to operate on the hard side. If we give too much to our soft side, we become the easy-going target—the one who won't do anything to hurt feelings and who allows people to manipulate them. Soft is good, but soft alone is bad. The same is true for hard. We need both. As I looked at myself and where I was, I put my work on a percentage basis so that I realized I spent 80 percent of my time and energy involved in the things to make the college run smoothly. The remaining 20 percent I spent dream releasing. That is, I was working 20 percent of my time on soft issues.

Only in looking back was I able to realize it, but that's when the first seeds of godly dissatisfaction were sown. I wanted to be able to spend 95 percent of my time dream releasing and 5 percent doing other things. *How could I make that possible?*

CHAPTER SIX
PASSION RETURNS

WHEN WE DISCOVER the right direction, passion returns. Until then, it's as if we've been living in a dead zone. We're bored or uneasy and nothing fills us with deep fulfillment and joy.

Once I knew where I wanted to go, I came alive again. In the months after I resigned from Beulah Heights, people would look at me and say things such as, "You look so refreshed." "Are you taking a break? Are you taking a vacation?"

I smiled and thanked them. I was refreshed—inwardly—because I was on the right ladder. Physically, my new life became more demanding. Yesterday I was in Chicago and tomorrow I'll be in St. Louis. I regularly speak in 100 to 150 places each year.

Even at the times when I'm physically tired, there is fire in my eyes. I love my life; I love what I'm doing.

The passion has returned. That's what they responded to. The new passion is there because I know where I want to go and I race up the new ladder. As tired as I am, I have no problem getting up in the morning. I stay excited because every day is a new challenge. I want to get moving each day because I have to find out how exciting it will be.

•••

One of the reasons the passion returned was because I was able to do more as a dream releaser. By that, I mean more inwardly satisfying things. Observers would say I did more at Beulah Heights. They had only to point out what had transpired at the campus. Not one inch of the entire grounds is the same as it was in 1989. Everything has changed.

That's not the kind of activity I mean. Today, my accomplishments show in the lives, attitudes, and activities of leaders. I sometimes say I help others leverage their own experiences. I had reached the place where I had enough life experiences and insight that I could help others climb their ladders. I've made mistakes in life that others don't need to make. I've also learned from those mistakes.

One day I had a conversation with a pastor in the Midwest. He's 28 years old, with a congregation of about 7,000 people. He's bright, charismatic, and a man of great vision. He has become one of my clients.

"You're going places. In just a few years, you're going to be a leading voice in this country," I said. "I can see only one thing that will stop you: Pride. If you allow pride to come in, that weakness may show through arrogance, a haughty spirit, or you start looking down on others. It can happen so easily—and I've seen it many times. Success has come your way early in life. You're going to face issues and situations that I didn't face until I was fifty. The mayor will call you for advice and you'll be involved in ribbon-cutting ceremonies. You'll receive more invitations for speaking engagements, and important people from foreign countries will invite you to speak. That's also the danger point."

I said that because I had messed up in that area. There was a period—and I'm glad it was a brief period—when I made those mistakes. When success smiled on me, I started to believe what others said. When people introduced me, I listened to all the wonderful praises.

Perhaps it sounds strange, but those wonderful, exhilarating things they say are true as long as we don't believe them. When we start to believe them, we lose them.

I said all those things and shared my experiences with that young pastor. I could say them gently and out of the soft side of myself, because I had been there. Because of my own bad judgment in the past, I could pass on some wisdom that I learned.

I want to help others become the best they can. I want to help them release their dreams. For me, success is to make others successful.

• • •

With the return of passion, I also focused more clearly. That is, I turned my energies toward doing more of the best things. As president, I had been involved in almost every aspect of the school.

I was involved in our accreditation.

I was a fund raiser.

I helped set up curriculum.

When financial aid issues came up, I was the one who got involved.

The list seemed to go on and on. Now was the time to concentrate on the areas where I wanted to work. I delegated responsibilities and resigned from organizations or asked others on the staff, especially Dr. Karanja, to replace me. That allowed me to do more in one area. I concentrated on what I wanted most to do: leadership.

That's all I do now.

When pastors move from one church to another, they won't be doing less in the new situation. Because of their experience, they will go into a new church being more focused. If I had gone from one church to another, I would have said to the board, "In my previous congregation, I did all the eighteen things that pastors can do. But here, I'm going to focus on leadership development and I'll do strong expository preaching. I did all kinds of counseling at the other church. But I'm not going to do counseling anymore." I would explain that even though counseling was something I could do, I had no passion for it. At least not on the same level as leadership development.

When I prepared to step off my old ladder, I said, "I don't want to work less; I want to put my energies into a narrower focus."

Here's another way passion works. Someone said ministers ought to accept a call to a church with the idea that they will stay there the rest of their lives. That doesn't mean that they will, but it means that being a pastor is exciting enough that they can envision staying there until retirement.

Here's a question leaders need to ask when they move from one position to another: Am I passionate enough right now that I can envision staying at this job for the rest of my professional life? Or is this only temporary? If it's only temporary, what are my motives for saying yes to the job?

In my case, I don't consider what I do as a job. It is, of course, and I get paid. But I think of what I do in terms of personal fulfillment and satisfaction that I have helped other people.

When we're passionate about our work, we may not be in the right place, but it's a good indication that we're moving in the right direction.

CHAPTER SEVEN
WHAT I WANT

I FACED BIG QUESTIONS in making the transition. What am I looking for? What do I need to find fulfillment? After months of self-searching, I settled on four things.

1. Independence. I had never been independent before and this would be a new experience for me. No one would know— or care—if I started to work at 6:00 or not until noon.

I had to ask myself: Can I work independently? I've functioned in structured situations all my life. Even when I was a pastor, there was some structure. I had hours at my discretion, but I had sermons to preach and lessons to teach, board meetings to conduct, visitation, baptisms, weddings, and funerals.

I asked myself one question: Do I like myself well enough to be alone all the time? Can I spend time with just me? I had never done that. When I went to the office, there were people in and out all day. Some days I received forty phone calls. How would I react when I received only two in a week? No longer would anyone stop by my office and ask if I wanted coffee or if I wanted to go out for lunch.

I have a beautiful office in my home. It's nicer than the one I had in the school, but nobody comes to see me. I have never had one client there, and I won't.

Could I live with that amount of independence?

I can and I have, but it was an adjustment—and I knew it would be. Now I can truly say I love the quiet of my office.

2. *Control.* Do I need outside control or do I have enough inner strength to traverse the journey with self-control? Do I have the self-discipline, accountability, and integrity? Do I need outside energy or an authority figure to tell me what to do or do I have what it takes? Can I get up in the morning if I don't have to keep office hours? Will I write that letter? Will I respond to that e-mail?

That one didn't trouble me because I've always been a self-starter.

3. *Freedom.* For me, this is different from independence. I had freedom at Beulah Heights. I could come and go and the board fully understood—but I produced results. They didn't care so long as I brought in results.

I wanted to enjoy my freedom—my ability to choose the people to work with and to turn down those I didn't want to work with.

Here's an added dimension to the matter of freedom: Can I handle it when my income depends on the amount of freedom I demand? Freedom versus income. If I'm not careful, the need for income will destroy my freedom because I'll rush from project to project, afraid that I'll go bankrupt if I don't get the next job.

4. *Structure.* I needed some kind of structure, but what kind? I use that word to explain how I would organize myself. Once

I've decided that I was okay on the control issue, what kind of structure did I need to set up my business?

Immediately I set myself up as not-for-profit and for-profit corporations with board members. Would that be enough? How often would I need to meet with them? What kind of reports should I make?

During that time, one verse in the Bible gave me immense peace, because I had sought God's will and I believed I was doing the right thing. "The Lord shall preserve your going out and your coming in. From this time forth and even forevermore" (Psalm 121:8, NKJV).

As I struggled with those four issues, I also asked myself: What are my core values? Who is the quintessential Samuel Chand? If anyone probed deeply enough, what values would they see that truly guide my life?

Some things are important to us at our core—our inner being—and others matter because they're important to our culture, our corporation, our community, or our family. It's not always easy to distinguish between core values and important concerns. It's easy to convince ourselves the valuables that are important to our organizations or our churches are those we love and must, thus, be of equal importance to us. When relationships tend to go bad, it's often because of a confusion between core values and important concerns.

I've already mentioned some of this, but increasingly, I saw that my value was as simple as the words of Jesus. He said that the first command was to love God totally and the second "is like it," that is, it is of equal importance. "You shall love your neighbor as yourself" (Matthew 22:39, NKJV).

I thought of it this way: If I zealously do what I can to enable others to look good—to be their best—isn't that one way of fulfilling the words of Jesus? If I help a pastor, I help the whole church; if I help a CEO, I'll help the whole organization.

I also realized how true this was with a little illustration. Suppose God said to me, "Make a choice. If you enter the first door, you'll find twenty pastors in there waiting for your help. If you take the second door, you'll face twenty thousand Christians. Choose which group you want and I'll be with you."

That decision didn't require any reflection. I would answer, "I'll go for the twenty." That made me realize my core value.

There were other values, and, of course, that is only one. But to know—to acknowledge those core values—means we have to be in touch with ourselves, with our inner selves. For some people, it's extremely difficult to probe deeply.

The other problem I saw in the matter of core values is that some try to claim too many. My guess—based on my experience in working with leaders and examining my own heart— is that, at most, most of us have three to five core values. If we truly ponder this, we'll probably cut them down to three.

How do we discover those core values?

We do a great deal of soul searching—including checking on our own motives.

We ask ourselves, "What do I value most?"

We relentlessly probe: "What do I care about? What do I dream about? When I daydream, what are the values?"

All of us have strong needs for acceptance, love, and affirmation. They're stronger in some people than they are in others. They're certainly part of the core issues we struggle with.

CHAPTER EIGHT
WHAT AM I LEAVING BEHIND?

F I SWITCH LADDERS, what am I leaving behind? At first, we think only of leaving, of finding a new perspective, or regaining our enthusiasm and zeal. Somewhere on our steps down that ladder, we have to look at ourselves and our work. Even in those instances of a bad experience, we can still find things we regret leaving.

When I started to think about what I was leaving, one of the first things I thought about was my legacy. Over the years, I've visited churches and companies where they have a gallery of pictures of their past leaders. They rarely show anything except a picture of the person and the years they served.

I know one church that does it differently. They have existed since 1853. Although it's in a fairly small city and the church never had a membership larger than 350, they did one significant thing to honor the legacy of their leaders. Under each picture, in three or four paragraphs, they list that pastor's achievements. The first pastor had founded the church because he believed in freeing slaves. Members pledged themselves to actively support emancipation. Three pictures from the end is a red-headed minister who volunteered as a chaplain in 1942—only weeks after World War II began. He died in the Normandy Invasion in 1944.

That's the way organizations need to work. Instead of denying or burying evidence of those who led, those who follow need to appreciate their legacy.

I began thinking about my legacy. *What am I leaving behind?* I asked myself. I don't know if anyone will even remember my name thirty years from now. That's not my point. I want to leave a legacy that shapes the future of the school. Whether I receive credit in the long term isn't important. It is important that I leave with a sense of accomplishment behind me.

Some days I pause and think, I've been more blessed than any human being can imagine. I had come to the United States as a foreigner whose English was sometimes difficult to grasp, who didn't understand many American customs or expressions, and God has given me such great favor. Even though I knew it was time to leave and my zeal had waned, my gratitude had not.

One day I said aloud to myself, "The kind of legacy I want to leave is a mark in human hearts."

I realized that I wanted to know there would be those who would say things such as:

"Without the influence of Sam Chand, I wouldn't have made it."

"Sam believed in me; and I learned to believe in myself."

"I wanted to work for God, but I had no idea what it was. Sam helped me see my potential. God used him to take me where I am today."

Because of that yearning for a human legacy, the urge became even stronger to move from behind the desk to sit across from people.

•••

I also wondered: Can I live without my present professional identity? *Will my influence be limited? Will it continue or diminish?*

While I was president, I could pick up the phone and I was two calls away from any leader. I didn't know if that would continue. My identity had been that of president of Beulah Heights Bible College. Before I became president, we used to say that the college was one of the nation's best-kept secrets. But now, at least in certain circles, Beulah Heights is recognized as a forward-thinking college and has proven invaluable to the community.

At my resignation ceremony, Bishop Eddie Long said, "We all need to recognize that Dr. Chand is Beulah Heights. No one talks about Beulah Heights without referring to Dr. Chand."

Naturally, I loved hearing those words, but that would be the past. I wouldn't be president any more. New questions arose in my mind:

What am I giving up along with that position?

Will people return my phone calls?

Will they continue to recognize me?

Now that I can't do something for them as I had before, will I still be significant in their lives?

Here's another question: Have I been significant to people because of who I am or for what I do? Most of us are afraid to ask ourselves that because the truth says, "It's because of what I do."

I had fearful feelings of walking away from everything I've worked for and built up. At Beulah Heights Bible College, there is not one square inch of that entire property that is the same. That wasn't easy to leave, because brick and mortar have a way of defining us. This is my house. It places me and I have somewhere to take people that is physical and tangible. And then it's gone. Now what?

I asked myself, suppose I was just a Christian who came into a church, sat in the back row every Sunday for four months. Then I missed three Sundays in a row. Who would call me? Would anyone e-mail or write to me? Would anyone care if I wasn't there?

The answer is that nobody would call and nobody would care. However, if I missed one Sunday as pastor, of course, everybody would want to know what was wrong. I thought, It's easy to see my worth because I'm on the payroll and employed by the church. If that's all there is, when I'm no longer there, does that mean I'm nothing?

It does unless I have grasped that my real value is internal and not just what I do for others.

When people talk about how important I am, I often smile and say, "Let me tell you what the conversation will be fifteen minutes after my funeral. The questions will go along this line: 'Where's the potato salad? What happened to all the beans?'"

I may have said it lightly, but I didn't take it lightly. When we leave a position of leadership—senior elder, CEO, vice-president, or pastor—we leave something behind. Ask pastors' widows; they know. They were the center of the church life one month, and the next they were pushed to the side. Of course, they were no longer the pastors' wives, but too often, they become people without identity.

I didn't want to leave Beulah Heights without a sense of identity or feeling I had left the best part of myself behind. I wanted to leave with the idea that I was enhancing my identity and my sense of self-worth.

• • •

Will the organization be able to sustain what I have started? Who and what is the organization going to lose because of my exit? Like a pastor who receives a call to a different congregation, I had to ask, "If I leave, who else will leave? Who will the school lose?"

I think that's more true for nonprofit organizations than for profit corporations. And yet in many large corporations when the top person leaves, there is often a big shake-up. In 2004, it happened with the Coca Cola Company in Atlanta. One of their major vice presidents left because the board had bypassed him and not selected him as the next president.

In many churches, when the senior pastor leaves a lot of staff leave. In some denominations such as the Assemblies of God, after the senior pastor leaves and a new pastor comes in, everyone on staff resigns. The new leader doesn't have to accept the resignations, but at least they're there, and provide an opportunity to make changes.

• • •

What am I leaving behind? In answering that question, I also realized the importance of relationships that I would leave behind. No matter how much I liked some of the people I worked with, my moving would mean they would have to change. Some people can push them away because there is always someone else to relate to. I value those long-term relationships. I had developed a number of them and wanted to maintain them. I also realized that some of them would have to be on a different level.

For example, Dr. James Keiller had been the dean of Beulah Heights when I enrolled as a student, and he is still a vital part of the college. He has been a good friend to me. We talked every day. Most of the conversations weren't about big things, but we talked.

Now what? Did I pull away from Dr. Keiller because I was leaving the school? I didn't want to do that, and I certainly didn't want to lose his friendship. But I knew it would mean relating on a different level.

He and I are still friends, we won't be as close as we were—and I knew that would happen. Part of our closeness had come about because we saw each other every day. When I first became president, our offices were across the hall from each other. I don't see Dr. Keiller often, but he's still important to me and I know I could go to him any time and our friendship would be intact.

Even though I knew my switching ladders would change our relationship, that realization of the shift in our relationship didn't make it easier. In a way, it was as if he had been on the same ladder and now I was climbing a different one. I could wave to him from my position, but our relationship was different.

CHAPTER NINE
TRANSITIONS AND GOD'S WILL

WHERE DOES GOD'S WILL FIT into this realm of transition? This certainly isn't the last question or the least important, but it was something I struggled over a great deal. As I pondered, I was reminded of Tim Elmore's four ways in which God speaks to us.

One is the thunderbolt. This is like Paul being knocked down on the road to Damascus or God speaking three times in a dream to Samuel.

Can God speak that way? Absolutely.

Does God often speak that way? Probably not.

Two is the call from birth. In the Old Testament, there were people called Nazirites, such as Samuel and Samson. In the New Testament era, John the Baptist probably fits into that category. From the time of their births, their parents dedicated them to God's service. For those children, choice was no option. They grew up knowing what God wanted and expected of them.

Third is a slow, growing awareness. It's not an immediate reaction and may take many years to unfold. It's like a latent talent. It's there all along, but it's hidden deeply within until we discover its presence. It's like someone who enjoys music but never played an instrument until she was twenty-five. Once her fingers touched the keyboard, something began to stir within her. The more she practiced, the better she became. If she hadn't had the latent ability, no amount of practice would have made her good.

That's how I felt about moving from my comfortable ladder. I had been in my position fourteen years. Only gradually did I become aware that I had abilities and gifts within me that were *beyond* being president. I used the word *beyond* and not *better than.* It's not a matter of comparing, but it's about obedience and being the person God calls us to be. My situation reminds me of Paul's discussion of spiritual gifts (1 Corinthians 12-14). He points out that the Holy Spirit equips for the good of all and it's not our business to compare. Our task is obedience.

One more thing about growing awareness is this. I believe that when we are following the Holy Spirit's guidance, we have peace ruling in our hearts. When we try something new, do it well, and enjoy it, that's a strong indication of God's plan gradually unfolding in our lives.

Four is that we see open doors. When I began the transition from president, I relied on the combination of three and four. I looked back over my life and asked, "Where have I been? What have I liked most? What has given me the greatest fulfillment in my service for God?"

Then I stared at the doors open to me.

I can always walk out of a room but I can't always walk into a room. I can always say no but I can't always say yes. If a door opens to me, I believe my responsibility is to peek inside. I may not know if it's God's will, but investigating the open door won't hurt.

When doors opened for me before I was ready to leave Beulah Heights, I didn't automatically dismiss them. Mentally, I opened each door and looked inside. In each instance, I sensed it wasn't the right door, so I could turn down the opportunity.

They were all great opportunities—but they weren't my opportunities.

For me, God's will has always been a fuzzy issue. I can't boil it down like some people who have an instant, easy formula. How he speaks to others is different from the way he speaks to me. I don't know a great deal about God's will, but I have learned to know the wavelength or frequency on which the Spirit communicates with me.

As we reflect on God's movement in our lives, here's a good question to ask: Do I know how God speaks to me? (Many people don't know the answer.)

The tendency for most of us—and I'm no exception—is that we always want to *know* or at least to *understand* God's will and ways. I've heard so many people quote Romans 8:28. ("And we know that all things work together for good to those who love God, to those who are the called according to His purpose.") Then they add, "Someday we'll understand." Maybe we won't—not ever. When we're seeking God's will we keep saying, "Show me. Tell me. Speak to me." If we really knew, we wouldn't be walking by faith. Perhaps that's why that greeting card in Omaha spoke powerfully to me:

That's living a life of faith: It happens when we have a growing sense of God's guidance and doors opening to us—especially doors we hadn't expected to open. That's when we close our eyes and leap.

The Danish theologian Soren Kierkegaard insisted that the highest good is to find our vocation (or calling) in life. He spoke of discerning God's will through using personal experience (growing awareness) and our convictions (open doors or obvious opportunities).

For me, once I sensed the direction God was taking me, I needed to take Kierkegaard's leap of faith—to jump into the unknown—and trust God's hands to grab me. I lead with my heart and my head has to follow. This isn't the method for everyone, but it's how I sense God at work in *my* life.

Here's one more way for people to see the Holy Spirit at work in their lives. I ask them to review their own spiritual journey. Look at all the significant moments in their lives. As they do so, I urge them to ask themselves:

Where are God's footprints in my life?

What divine patterns can I see?

How does the Lord speak most often to me?

What were the last three major decisions I made? What were the common factors in all of them?

• • •

Where does living on the edge by faith play a role? There's an old saying, "If we're living on the edge, we're taking up too much room."

That means we need to keep moving. The edge needs to become edgier. There is no such place where we can stand and say, "This is the edge," because the edge is always extending itself. Otherwise, eventually the edge becomes our comfort zone.

CHAPTER TEN
TRANSITION ISSUES

O NCE I MADE the public announcement of my leaving, I felt scared and excited at the same time. I'd wake up in the middle of the night in a cold sweat. Some speak of butterflies in their stomach, I only know my mind immediately filled with questions that nagged at me:

What if I'm making a mistake?

What if I can't pay my bills? If I can't pay the mortgage?

What if all these people who are saying they will pay me don't come through?

What if a church leader says, "We've just had three bad months and we can't keep paying you"?

What if I'm not in control of anything? At the college I was in control and I could make things happen.

Just as powerful were the dreams and positive thoughts. They are what kept me going during those times of uncertainty:

I can help others succeed.

I can work directly with people who need my expertise.

I can awaken dreams and show others how to bring those dreams to reality.

I can help leaders think through transitional issues.

I thought of it this way: The wider the banks of the river, the slower the water. It has a kind of lazy, drifting effect. The narrower the river, however, means the narrower the gorge, but the same volume of water has to flow through the narrow banks. That means the water must go deeper. It also means the momentum builds and those in the river can't just coast. We are rushing downstream. My task was to take the wide banks of the river and narrow them.

Using this analogy, the river starts as a gushing spray or waterfall. That's *passion*. The passion continues as long as the river gushes. In time, the force of the water causes the banks to widen, the river flattens. Eventually the river becomes a slow, lazy drifter. For the river to regain power—call it momentum or passion—the banks have to become narrow again. Sometimes engineers make this happen and the river moves forcefully once again. That's how I see passion at work.

•••

There are no smooth transitions, because smooth means everything goes exactly as planned. There are only good transitions or poorly executed ones. Of course, I wanted a seamless changeover, but I knew better. We always face the IBs-the inevitable bumps. Our best-laid plans usually don't work out. Therefore, I aimed for an effective transition. And we did hit a few IBs.

What were they?

I expected everyone to understand where I was in my life. I naively believed that if I explained, they would understand.

I expected everyone to truly want things to work out well for me.

I expected almost everyone to applaud my decision and my courage to try a new path.

I smile about it now, but it wasn't an easy time for me. We can talk to ten people and nine can be affirming, but if one person isn't, that response is the one we tend to remember and focus on. Long ago, I learned to tune out those negative voices. I have learned that when I plan new programs I need to listen to the negative voices and evaluate their objections. But when I plan for my life, I have to listen to God and to my own heart and forget the negative voices.

My biggest bump happened before I announced my resignation. This took place in August and I didn't plan to announce my resignation until October.

I had gone with a large group of a hundred plus people to Nakuru, Kenya, East Africa. One Sunday we were in the Nakuru Deliverance Church with thousands of people present. Bishop Mark Kariuki escorted me up to speak. Dr. Benson Karanja sat in the front row.

As I stood on the platform, I stared at Dr. Karanja, and it was as if a voice whispered to me, "Tell them about Dr. Karanja." Immediately, another part of me censored that idea. I was greeting the people, but in the back of my head, an argument went on. I can't announce my leaving, I argued. What if the news gets back to Atlanta?

But the voice inside pushed me. "He is from Nakuru, Kenya. You will never have a second opportunity to position him in his own country like the one you have right now. The next time he'll already be president, but you can increase his value in their eyes right now."

While I talked, I also stalled for time while I processed what I should say. Then I said to myself, "Go for it."

I told the people that I was going through a major transition and I would resign from Beulah Heights. As I said those words,

I saw the surprised expressions on faces of three of my faculty members in the front row.

"I have a great announcement to make." I paused and took a deep breath. This was a big step of faith for me. The board not only hadn't acted on my resignation—they didn't even know of it. "The next president of Beulah Heights Bible College is not going to come from America. He is not coming from India. He's going to come from Kenya." I paused and said slowly, "He is not just coming from Kenya, but from Nakuru."

By now, they filled the building with praise and shouts of thanksgiving.

"And the next president of Beulah Heights Bible College will be Dr. Benson Karanja!" I called him forward.

As Dr. Karanja came forward, pandemonium broke out for nearly fifteen minutes. During that time I asked myself, what have I done? At the school, we had more than a hundred students from Kenya, mostly from Nakuru. All of them had families that were in that church. The pastor's sister-in-law, Hannah Mariuki, was on our staff. The news would travel to Atlanta before I got back. (That happened. By the time I returned, they had received a video of my making that announcement in Kenya.)

As soon as I returned to Atlanta, I called one of the leaders of the Kenya students and told them that I felt I had to make that announcement in Nakuru. "Please keep this to yourselves. You can talk freely after October 15." They promised to keep quiet.

For a month and a half, they kept it to themselves. That was very kind of them. That was the biggest bump, but we survived.

• • •

Everything rises and falls on transitions—passing of the baton. Races have been lost after the baton has been passed. I had to work carefully so nobody would doubt that Dr. Karanja had my blessings. I couldn't be half-hearted in that. In this case, it worked out because I really was totally for him.

But I still had to make the transition. What files did I turn over? When did I turn them over? I made computer copies of everything for him. I went over everything with him. I spent hours with him making certain he understood everything I had done. Even if he didn't agree with my position on everything, I wanted him to understand why I did things the way I did. The transition worked because I knew the person who would follow.

We don't always know. For example, most pastors aren't allowed to pick their successors. If I were in that position I would contact the successor once that person has started the job. "I'll be happy to turn over any transitional issues," I would say. "We can do it one of two ways or we can do it both ways. I have everything that I think you need, and what you don't need you can throw away. I can bring that to you and we can go over everything. Or during the next few days, you can make a list of the things you need from me. Or if you decide you don't want anything from me, that's okay too."

Handing over was especially significant to me. When I became president of Beulah Heights, my predecessor left me nothing. Everything I learned was anecdotal. He was already gone but there was nothing left—no files to go through or records of commitments or a list of responsibilities. He may have been trying to give me free reign and not depend on his policies, but I didn't know anything. For me, every day was on-the-job training with no rules or guidelines to follow.

•••

There is one other issue, that of being a lame duck. How do we to stay productive during the lame-duck period? This was a big issue for me to cope with. I had resigned in the middle of October and I would have two-and-a-half months left at the school. The good thing is the college closed for Thanksgiving week and after the second week of December students would be gone, so it was down time. In my research, I discovered that almost all college presidents announced their resignation long in advance and actually resigned June 30, because the fiscal year for all colleges begins in July, and they had no down time. That's one of the reasons why I timed it as I did.

I didn't want to be lame duck too long. Not just for their sake but for my sake. I had mentally packed my bags and my heart was no longer at the school. It wasn't fair to them for me to stay.

• • •

How much notice should I give with my resignation? When I left my church to go to Beulah Heights, I gave them too much notice—six months. That was not good. This time I gave two-and-a-half months' notice but I had a Thanksgiving and Christmas built into it.

I'm not referring to retirement, because that is different. I think people need to wrestle and struggle with the right amount in their context. In most cases, anything more than a month might be too long. Many pastors have told me the last week can get very long. "Each Sunday it gets harder because I'm looking toward the future while I have to focus on the present," one pastor said.

• • •

How do we maintain organizational morale in times of leadership transitions? How do we slow the seepage? This is a time when those who are peripheral and borderline start to seep away. They became involved with Beulah Heights because of me. Some donors, for example, gave because they liked me but not because of their commitment to the school.

So I had to do many one-on-one conversations—a lot of phone calls, a lot of building up of Dr. Karanja. I had to take him to luncheon and breakfast meetings and other places that he had never been to and introduce him as the next president. I had to make sure that I walked the room with him and, in effect, to show that he had my blessings. I'd learned that when a pastor chooses to resign, we need to ask, "Who else is going to leave?" That was even more important to ask in this situation.

I didn't want any of our donors and friends to slip away. Dr. Karanja and I worked faithfully to show them that the school wasn't going down, that I totally supported him, and that our vision hadn't changed.

• • •

What about loyalty issues? This was more on the mind of those employed by the college, so I freed them up. I said to them at our staff meeting on October 15, "Dr. Karanja's office is right behind mine. There's nothing that will make me feel better than for you to walk past my office," I said, "and go to Dr. Karanja from now on."

It was the right thing to do, and they started doing exactly what I told them to do. My words sounded right, but it wasn't that easy for me. The problem is I felt useless and pushed aside. "What am I doing here?" I had to keep in mind that they had not been disloyal, but they were being functional.

Yesterday I was president and they came to me, now I'm not the president so they go to the one who can answer them.

CHAPTER ELEVEN
PROCESSING INFORMATION

PEOPLE PROCESS INFORMATION differently, and men don't usually process the same as most women. I'm making a generalization here, of course, because it's not just a gender matter. In my experience at Beulah Heights, I saw this largely divided that way.

Generally speaking, I found women more open to transitions than men. Women on my staff seemed much more resilient and affirming. They were able to see my larger picture before the men could. The men tended to bog down in the pragmatic end. "What's going to happen to the school?" they asked.

Women tend to ask *feeling* questions while men ask *doing* questions. Women ask, "How is that going to affect me?" Men ask "How is that going to affect the organization?"

The women reflected on my leaving and said, "We're going to miss you as a friend." Men were more concerned about, "We're going to miss you as our leader."

The women asked relational questions, and at the time I was making my transitions, those questions, which showed the soft side of leadership, were more important to me. In the days following my announcement, women asked:

"How are you doing, Dr. Chand?"

"How are you feeling?"

"How's the family doing? How's Brenda doing? What did the girls say?"

"Will you still come by and see us sometime?"

Men focused on the practical issues that troubled them:

"Who's going to sit in which office?"

"How will this affect contributions?"

"Will this decrease student enrollment?"

"What's your web site going to say?"

As departing leaders, we want to have both types of responses. It helps us remain aware that we're moving in different contexts. Two simultaneous tracks are running. If we're looking for one and get the other, we don't need to feel bad about the person, that's where he or she is.

CHAPTER TWELVE
THE FINAL RUNG

HAD REACHED THE FINAL RUNG. It was time for me to leave. December 31 was an awkward day for me. Dr. Benson Karanja was waiting to move into my office; I was waiting for staff to leave so I could walk out of the building without having to speak to anyone. I didn't want to face a group of people when I closed the door behind me. I had already removed the equipment so the office was bare except for my laptop and a few papers on top of my desk. (I still had a few files—part of my stalling technique.)

Just before noon, I sent an e-mail to the entire staff, saying that on the last day in office the President of the United States usually pardons people. "My last act as your president is this: You may all go home today at 2:00 p.m."

Then I called in Dr. Karanja and turned over everything to him. The last thing I handed him was my keys. We hugged and I told him, "I'll be out of here in a few minutes." I spent about two minutes by myself in my office, emotionally preparing myself to leave.

Finally, I opened the door that led to the parking lot. I turned the knob to lock the door and pulled it closed behind me.

I heard the click of the lock.

The final click said to me, "There is no going back. You're leaving. When you drive away from here, you're gone. You no longer belong here."

To my amazement, I hadn't been emotionally prepared for that finality. The hard side of me had done everything and the transition had gone fine; the soft side wasn't quite ready to admit finality. I wasn't prepared to hear the click of the door. I wasn't ready to stand outside the office door and say to myself, "Your feet are going to take you only in one direction. There are no U-turns here."

Of course, I've moved on, but that one moment was also the moment of reality. After fourteen years, I had stepped off that ladder.

• • •

"How are Dr. Karanja and the college doing?" I hear that question often. My answer: "Better than ever." That's true. At the writing of this book, the college has experienced three semesters under Dr. Karanja's leadership, with record enrollment, strong finances, high morale, and renewed vision.

CHAPTER THIRTEEN
PREPARING OUR SUCCESSORS

THE MOST GIFTED athletes rarely make good coaches. The best violinist will not necessarily make the best conductor. Nor will the best teacher necessarily make the best head of the department.

"So it's critical to distinguish between the skill of performance and the skill of leading the performance, two entirely different skills.

In "Spotting New Leaders" in *Christianity.com* (April 18, 2004), Fred Smith writes, "It's also important to determine whether a person is capable of learning leadership. The natural leader will stand out. The trick is identifying those who are capable of learning leadership over time."

In my previous book, *Who's Holding Your Ladder*, I addressed the differences between leaders and managers. Let's look at the characteristics of potential leaders. As we take steps toward leaving, part of our responsibility is to ensure that the organization flows without us. If we do a good job of preparing for our successor, the organization will flourish.

One way we make sure the organization doesn't falter after we leave is to seek potential leaders to fill the vacant spots. We need to appreciate those we already have and give them greater visibility if their deeds call for it.

As we work with them (as I did with Dr. Karanja), we also need to reach out for others who are just starting their climb up the ladder.

Here are a few things I've learned in the process.

Instead of saying, "This is bad," and being negative, potential leaders usually say, "There must be a better way." The best of them eventually come up with a better way. Managers or non-leaders shrug and say, "Maybe it's not the best, but it works."

Good leaders are imaginative, but they are also practical. They sense what can happen. They're the kind who can listen to ideas and instinctively say, "This will work" or "This won't work." They can usually explain why.

The best leaders recognize others' good ideas and encourage them. They don't have to be the source of all wisdom.

One pastor used to have two overnight retreats each year with all elected elders, but he also invited a handful of others—active members who showed potential. He invited them by saying, "We'd like your input." He called it Church Leaders' Retreat. He carefully chose the potential leaders: They were individuals who had begun to emerge in leadership roles.

One time he asked the people at the retreat to dream of what they would like to see happen at the church within the next year. "Make it something that's practical and achievable if we put the resources behind it." He gave them plenty of time to think and then wrote their responses on a chalkboard. They had fourteen items.

When they finished, they spent a few minutes discussing each dream—not to cut out anything but to make the concept clear to everyone. When possible, he combined ideas because they seemed to work together. They ended up with nine items.

"I don't want to push away any good ideas," he said, "so here's what I'd like to do. Think through these ideas and I'd like you to volunteer to explore the idea. That's all—just explore. Is this a good idea? Is it possible? Will it work? Is it something our church needs to be doing? You do not have to take on that task if we approve it. All we want you to do is to be part of a committee to consider the possibilities." He said a committee could be two people or five. They could also be part of more than one group but no more than three.

Within minutes, those present had volunteered for all nine. He then asked if anyone had not volunteered for a project to choose at least one.

A month later, they had a meeting at the church, and each of the groups made a short report. They assigned each suggestion (and its report) to an ad hoc committee of the church board with the stipulation they could use non-elders to see if the committee felt any of the ideas were workable. Not all the ideas were feasible. A few were too far down the road for them to explore in depth.

The pastor saw the event as important because it kept new ideas flowing and encouraged members to think creatively. It was also an opportunity to watch potential leaders in action. Some of them were excellent at what they did, such as teach, sing, or organize church suppers, but they didn't have that extra spark to move into stronger leadership positions. The elders, who served three-year terms, could see their potential replacements.

●●●

Here's another thing I've learned about choosing the right people: When leaders speak, people listen. They may not say a lot, but what they say is important.

Just as important is the respect leaders receive. Peer respect doesn't reveal ability; it reveals character and personality. As Christian businessman Maxey Jarman said, "It isn't important that people like you. It's important that they respect you. They may like you but not follow you. If they respect you, they'll follow you, even if perhaps they don't like you" (from "Spotting New Leaders" in *Christianity.com,* April 18, 2004).

I also believe we need to observe the family dynamic. How leaders behave at home speaks about their leadership, commitment, and integrity. Some leaders are never home. They're busy at the church but neglectful of their first responsibility—care of their own children. It doesn't take much observing to figure out the relationship within the family. If there is harmony, respect, and love, it shows. If those qualities aren't there, that shows too.

Another indicator of leadership potential is past experience. Here are questions to ask:

- What kind of leadership role have you had in the past?
- What do you consider your best achievements?
- What do you do when there is conflict between two people and you need to intervene?

For those who have no record of accomplishment, here are techniques to use:

1. Look at their completed work in previous employment or activities. It doesn't require much time to see how they acted in the past—regardless of whether it was in the church, on the job, or in volunteer programs. People reveal who they are by the way they behave.

The workplace and churches are filled with people who volunteer or agree to complete additional tasks but never seem to get them done. Watch for those who refuse to stop until they've completed everything they've agreed to do.

Observe their attitude while they're working.

Do they sense this is important?

Do they enjoy completing the task (even if it's not something they enjoy doing)?

When they complete a task, are they ready for a new one? (Some people hide from sight so they won't get "picked on" again.)

2. *Say, "Tell me about your vision of the future."* As you listen to their words, observe their gestures and body language, thus you can sense how they see what lies ahead.

3. *As you listen to them talk, also focus on their willingness to shoulder responsibility.* Are they eager to learn new skills? Do they willingly accept additional work and see it as a challenge?

In the mundane tasks, do they seek better ways to accomplish the same goals?

4. *Can they blend their human side with tough-mindedness, and do they know which side to work from at the appropriate time?* All leaders get criticized and have discouraging moments or times of failure. Potential leaders don't allow their feelings to interfere with doing a good job.

Do they know when to place people's needs before slavish regulations?

Can they say or do what's necessary to complete an unpopular task?

Can they ask for help when they need it, but stand on their own when they must?

CHAPTER FOURTEEN
CLIMBING THE NEW LADDER

A S LEADERS, THE actions we take during the first three months while we ascend our new ladders largely determine whether we succeed or fail. If we fumble during that time, we may be able to make up for it—but it won't be easy. We need to make the most of transitions—especially in those first three months.

Most people are aware that every time we elect a new president, a report comes out of his first 100 days in office—that's slightly over three months. It's a gauge to the nation of that president's effectiveness over the four-year period.

Transitions provide unique opportunities—chances to start afresh and make needed changes. Almost every leader knows that. What they often don't consider is that those first 90 days are also a period of acute vulnerability. During that period, they will establish working relationships and will define their roles.

In any job, there is something called "paying the rent." Those are the things that we absolutely must do. If I'm a pastor, I must preach Sundays, conduct baptisms and funerals, officiate at weddings, and moderate at board meetings. Thirty years ago, researchers figured that paying the rent is a half-time job. A large part of the pastors' mark (legacy) depends on what they do the other half of their work week. Some teach classes; others engage in political activities; some build programs or focus on evangelism. What they do after paying the rent is as important as the effectiveness with which they work.

In his book, *The First 90 Days: Critical Success Strategies for New Leaders at All Levels*, Michael Watkins, associate professor of the Harvard Business School, refers to the "breakeven point" (page 30). That is when new leaders have contributed as much value to their new organization as they have consumed from it. He also offers ten suggestions to face the transition challenges:

1. Make a definite, final, mental break from your old job.

2. Accelerate your learning.

3. Match strategy to situation (a clear diagnosis of the situation is essential).

4. Secure early wins to build credibility and create momentum.

5. Negotiate success with your boss by managing expectations.

6. Achieve alignment between organizational structure and its strategy.

7. Build or restructure your team.

8. Create coalitions or supportive alliances.

9. Keep your balance and your ability to make good judgments (the risk of losing perspective and making bad calls is ever present during transitions).

10. Help everyone in your organization to accelerate their own transitions and strengthen succession planning (leadership transition acceleration).

• • •

In an article published in April of 2004 by *Christianity Today.com,* Fred Smith lists 8 signs of leadership potential:

1. *Do I see a constructive spirit of discontent?* They are the ones who see better ways to get things done.

2. *Do they offer practical ideas?* Good leaders can judge the effect of ideas and say whether they will or will not work.

3. *Is anybody listening?* Smith points out that when potential leaders speak, others listen.

4. *Does anyone respect them?* Respect from peers doesn't show ability but it does imply character and personality.

5. Can they create or catch vision?

6. Do they show a willingness to take responsibility?

7. Do they finish the job?

8. *Are they tough-minded?* Smith points out that no one can lead without being criticized, but potential leaders need mental toughness to go through difficult times.

MOVING OUR LADDERS: WHEN MEMBERS LEAVE A CHURCH

A LMOST ALL OUR CHURCHES have some form of new-member classes. They usually do an excellent job of orienting new members to the church family. Few churches teach people how to leave a church. One of the pastors who does is Bishop Richard Hilton of Calvary Church in Elizabethtown, Tennessee. Much of what I'm writing comes from his pastor's class and is called "Avoiding Separation."

● ● ●

There is a way and a time to join a local church; there is also a way and a time to leave. Sometimes God sends people to a church for a period of time. It is possible that some people attend a church to learn certain things before they move on. Or they receive training and are sent out.

Sometimes it happens that problems or situations arise when members don't agree with the leaders—and I refer only to big issues. In any church, things go on that not everyone readily accepts. When the leaders of a congregation take a stand that members feel is significant and works against their principles, that may be time to leave.

We all know of instances of immorality within congregations. In one instance, there was strong evidence that a female choir member was having an affair with a deacon. Several members brought the matter up to the pastor and to the board and nothing happened. A number of families left the congregation before the leaders took any action.

There are other times:

Doctrinal error may slip in.

Job transfers occur.

Members move on another part of the city or a new city.

The church may take a new direction. (One congregation decided that because almost all of their members were over sixty, they would focus their activities on them. Most of the younger members moved elsewhere.)

Although there are definite times when people need to leave a congregation, there are correct ways to leave. If nothing else, they should leave as courteously as possible. The leaders deserve an explanation. Too many people simply disappear and end up at another church.

I've been with pastors at restaurants and they've seen a former member and they say hello. The former members left without telling anyone and they're usually embarrassed. Finally, they blurt out, "We decided to join Mt. Hope church." This is awkward for both of them, and such situations shouldn't have to take place.

My co-writer remembers a couple named Rosa and Al who asked to see him. They had decided to leave the church because they had become involved in a formal church. "We miss the liturgy and that style of worship," Al said. It was obvious he couldn't change their minds, so he gave them his personal blessings and prayed for the couple.

In one church I know, whenever anyone makes it known they are leaving, the elders have a farewell ceremony at the end of their final worship service. It lasts only a few minutes, but it involves a commendation to the departing family and a prayer. At that same church, before the family leaves, the pastor and at least one elder visit and ask them, "Is there any unfinished business? Any bad feelings? Any injured relationships?" If so, they pray and urge the departing members to attempt reconciliation whenever possible.

Bishop Hilton says, "If you leave the right way, you can come in the right way at the next church." By that he means if people leave on good terms they can start their new membership on good terms.

Staying together isn't easy. Whether we like it or not, divorce takes place around us all the time. In every relationship, it is vital to learn scriptural principles that enable us to avoid separation. We need to work at maintaining healthy, loving, and forgiving relationships within the church family. It's unfortunate, but many don't operate by principle but by feeling. If they feel slighted or offended, they act on those negative emotions. They do nothing to understand, reconcile, or forgive.

APPENDIX B
EXIT ETIQUETTE

N EW CHURCH MEMBERS understand entrance etiquette—how to join a church; however, few understand exit etiquette—how to leave a church.

1. There is a difference between membership and covenant. Membership is a necessity placed on groups to conduct business. It has responsibilities as well as privileges. As necessary as membership may be in our present society, it is not a biblical concept. The biblical concept is that of covenant, or being grafted or adopted into a family. The idea is that we don't merely join or become part of the church—we are the church—we are part of the family that worships in that building. Think how this applies to leaving. In a home when someone is leaving, common courtesy says that we notify someone of our departure, whereabouts and relating logistics—exit etiquette.

In a church, however, because many members don't understand covenant, they feel they can leave a church without following any protocol or exit etiquette. They fail to grasp the covenantal and familial biblical concepts.

Think of these three things:

1. More than a member, we are in covenant.
2. We are family members.
3. That is why we call it our home church.

Here are questions prospective and new members need to ask themselves.

1. Why am I here?
2. Is this going to be my home until the Lord moves me?
3. Does my personal passion coincide with the vision of this congregation?
4. Are there opportunities for me to use my God-given gifts?

There are legitimate reasons for leaving a church.

1. Geographical relocation that makes commuting to that church impractical.
2. Drastic change of vision in the church that may not be compatible with your reasons for joining.
3. Doctrinal heresy.
4. Being sent out by the church as a church planter, missionary, or evangelist.

Here are issues to consider when leaving a church.

1. Have I been brutally honest with myself?
2. Have I prayed diligently through this issue?
3. Have I followed the protocol and shared with those who have been given oversight of my well being? (These could be elders, deacons, cell leaders, departmental pastors or solo pastors.)
4. If it is because of conflict and controversy, have I verified all the facts directly from the source?

5. Do I hold unforgiveness in my heart?

6. Am I angry?

7. Am I leaving because it is my decision, or am I being negatively influenced?

8. Will I be a carrier of negativity from this church to the next church?

9. Am I leaving in such a way that I could return to this church family?

10. Have I been courteous?

11. Have I been respectful of godly authority?

12. Have I said negative things to others in the church?

13. What do I expect this church to do when I tell them I am leaving?

14. If I were the pastor or a senior leader in the church, what would I expect as exit etiquette from those choosing to leave?

There is an exit etiquette strategy.

1. Never leave with unresolved issues of anger, bitterness, or unforgiveness.

2. Always do your best to speak with those in oversight about your plans. Don't go AWOL.

3. Do not make a scene or production out of your leaving.

4. When you leave, leave. Do not keep meddling in the place you chose to leave.

5. Do not try to influence others to follow you in leaving.

6. Leave in such a way that your godliness will be exemplary, you will be missed, and you'll be welcomed back.

Here's the test of good exit etiquette strategy: If you see a church leader in a restaurant, grocery store, or bank is there awkwardness because of any unfinished business?

APPENDIX C
MY BACKWARD PLAN²

THE SIMPLE PREMISE of backward planning is that we define our prime objective, or a big goal that will move us toward our prime objective and assign it a date. As Henry Kimsey-House said, "A goal without a date is a dream."

Second, we need to figure out the next to last thing that needs to happen before our goal is met, and figure the time frame for that.

Then we ask, "What would need to happen before that?"

"And before that?"

• • •

By (date) _____ I will have achieved (Prime Objective) _____.

---

2. This is adapted from *Leverage Your Best Ditch the Rest* by Scott Blanchard & Madeleine Homan (New York: Wm. Morrow, 2004, page 30.

YOUR NEXT BOLD MOVE

Just prior to that (date) _____, I will need to have done _____
_____
_____.

And before that can happen (date) _____, I will need to have accomplished (milestone) _____
_____
_____.

To enable the next step on (date) _____ I will need to have (milestone) _____
_____
_____ in place.

By (date) _____ I will have done (milestone) _____
_____
_____
_____.

By (date) _____ I will have done (milestone) _____
_____
_____..

Today (or tomorrow) I will (milestone) _____
_____.

APPENDIX D
SEASONS OF DESTINY[3]

To EVERYTHING THERE is a season, a time for every purpose under heaven, There is a right time for everything" (Ecclesiastes 3:1, TLB).

FOUR SEASONS OF DESTINY

Starting season—Sovereign Foundations

Searching season—Starting out, Survival or Struggling

Successful season—Skill formation

Significant season—Convergence

NOTE 1

The length of seasons may vary but usually are from 15-20 years each

---

3. This section is used by permission from a teaching of Dr. Garnet Pike, Dean at Southwestern Christian University

NOTE 2

Between ages 30-55, critical incidents (positive or negative) will shape your life.

FIRST SEASON: SOVEREIGN FOUNDATIONS

Starting phase

- Providential—things you had no choice over such as:
- Place of birth, country, city, rural etc.
- Parents—home situation
- Nationality, ethnicity
- Color of hair, skin, bodily features
- Male or female

Leadership Beginnings

- Questioning
- Self worth—Do I matter?
- Confidence—Am I able?
- Abilities—Can I do it?
- Destiny & Purpose—Why was I placed on this planet?
- Relationship with God—Is this God's will?
- Call—Is this my life calling?
- Experimental Phase—What can I try?
- Ministry out of DOING—Competence and performance orientation.

SECOND SEASON

Searching, Survival, Struggling

- First steps of ministry
- Attempt various things in ministry
- Change jobs or ministry assignments often

- Rely on own gifts and persona
- Develop skills in ministry
- Ministry out of DOING—Competence and performance orientation.

THIRD SEASON

Success—focused ministry

Competence in ministry

Skill formation

Merging of role, gifting, competence and influence

Season of successes

Focused ministry

Role shift

Unique ministry

Ministry out of BEING—Security and personhood orientation.

FOURTH SEASON

Significance—Convergence in ministry

Shift from success to significance

Merging of role, giftedness and competence

Focus on Ultimate Contribution

Fulfill a sense of destiny

Wondering about Impact

Tombstone issues

Ministry out of BEING—Security and personhood orientation.

You know exactly how I was made, bit by bit, how I was sculpted from nothing to something. Like an open book, you watched me grow from conception to birth; all the stages of my life were spread out before you. The days of my life all prepared before I'd even lived one day (Psalm 139:15-16, The Message).

I know what I'm doing. I have it all planned out-plans to take care of you, not abandon you, plans to give you the future you hope for (Jeremiah 29:11, The Message).

For I know the thoughts and plans that I have for you, says the Lord, thoughts and plans for welfare and peace and not for evil, to give you hope in your final outcome (Jeremiah 29:11, Amplified).

"It's not so much that we are afraid of change or so in love with the old ways, but it's that place in between that we fear...It's like being between trapezes. It's Linus when his blanket is in the dryer. There is nothing to hold on to." — Marilyn Ferguson, American Futurist

CPSIA information can be obtained
at www.ICGtesting.com
Printed in the USA
FSHW020105140520